häfelinger + wagner

design

häfelinger + wagner
design gmbh

Türkenstraße 55–57
80799 München

HARD FACTS ON GOOD DESIGN.

kirsten DIETZ / *jochen* RÄDEKER

STRICHPUNKT

VERLAG HERMANN SCHMIDT MAINZ

40 projects. 20 theses. 1 manifesto.

People mostly judge design on whether they like it
or not. Although that is important, it is but one criterion.
That is why this book not only showcases our work,
but also sets out in twenty theses the basic principles of
what constitutes good design. Theses for an informed
discussion, which is necessary if design is to be more than
just pretty to look at. When designers understand their
career as not just a job, but an attitude.
This is what concerns us. This is what drives us.
This is what we believe in.
This is how we measure ourselves and let others
measure us.

However, in all sincerity, a thesis is always an ideal state
that we only seldom achieve, and in doing so remain
constantly unsatisfied. Before you is a manifesto whose
goals are barely achievable. And that is precisely why
it is so important.

We try harder. With every new job. With every new idea.
With every new design.
There is no path without a goal.
There is no success without failure.
There is no reward without hard work.

Good design is a tough job: go for it!

Kirsten Dietz & Jochen Rädeker

40 Projekte. 20 Thesen. 1 Manifest.

Design wird meist nur danach beurteilt, ob es gefällt
oder nicht. Das ist wichtig, aber nur ein Kriterium.
Deshalb zeigt dieses Buch nicht nur unsere Arbeiten,
sondern liefert in zwanzig Thesen die Grundlagen dafür,
was gutes Design ausmacht. Thesen für eine fundierte
Diskussion, die nötig ist, wenn Gestaltung nicht nur
hübsch sein soll. Wenn Designer ihren Beruf nicht als
Job, sondern als Haltung begreifen.
Das ist es, was uns umtreibt.
Das ist es, was uns antreibt.
Das ist es, woran wir glauben.
Das ist es, woran wir uns messen und messen lassen.

Eine These ist bei aller Ernsthaftigkeit aber immer auch
ein Idealzustand, den wir nur ganz selten erreichen,
bei dessen Umsetzung wir ständig unzufrieden bleiben.
Vor euch liegt ein Manifest, dessen Ziele kaum zu
erreichen sind. Und genau deshalb ist es so wichtig.

We try harder: Mit jedem neuen Job.
Mit jeder neuen Idee. Mit jedem neuen Entwurf.
Ohne Ziel kein Weg.
Ohne Scheitern kein Erfolg.
Ohne harte Arbeit kein Lohn.

Good design is a tough job: Go for it!

Kirsten Dietz & Jochen Rädeker

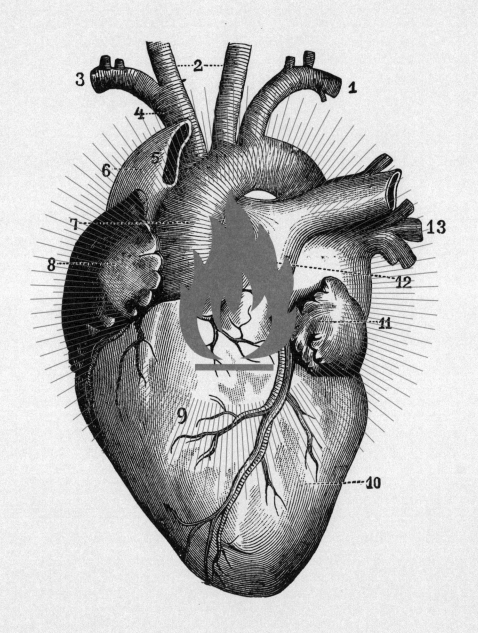

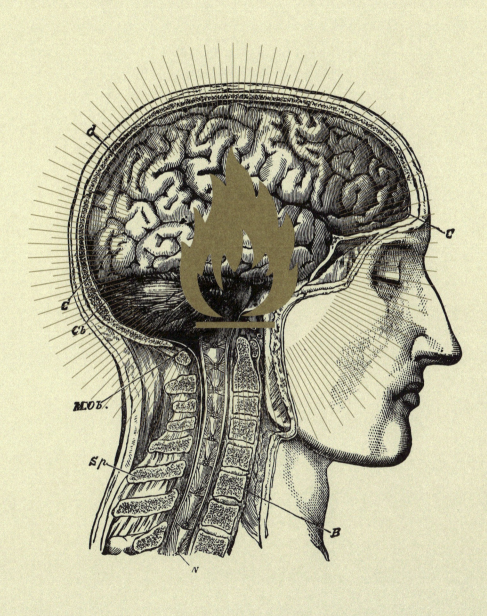

1.0 /

GOOD DESIGN IS NOT A JOB.

.01

If designing is your job, you are a hairdresser, decorator or a display trimmer. But not a designer. Good design is an attitude, not a job. It is the absolute will to change things sustainably using visual means, to make the world a fit place to live in. Your goal is to make headway, not to head off home: good design is a permanent challenge.

Wenn Design dein Job ist, bist du Friseur, Maler oder Schauwerbegestalter. Aber kein Gestalter. Gute Gestaltung ist eine Haltung, kein Beruf. Ist der unbedingte Wille, die Dinge mit visuellen Mitteln nachhaltig zu verändern, die Welt zu einem lebenswerten Platz zu machen. Dein Ziel heißt Verbesserung, nicht Feierabend: Gutes Design fordert dich permanent.

1.1 /

Corporate Design & series of posters
CLIENT _ RUHRTRIENNALE

(2009 – 2011)

PRIMAL
MOMENTS

There are only a few places in which people work as intensely as they do in the theatre. This is also true when it comes to designing how it looks. Yet despite working long days and nights, we didn't manage to finish the image for the RUHRTRIENNALE. But this was completely deliberate. The aim of the festival was to address the question as to what extent art and the religiousness of man have the same inner origin. So we came up with a sign in a paintbrush style that simultaneously depicts an 'R' (for Ruhr) and a '3' (for triennale) and deliberately looks *unfinished* – as is ultimately always the case with our debate on art and religion. Both on buildings as well as in the media, handwriting, motion blur and image decomposition represent the debate with world religions, the fun that is had as a designer, and the late nights at the office.

Es gibt nur wenige Orte, an denen intensiver gearbeitet wird als am Theater.
Das gilt auch, wenn es um die Gestaltung des Auftritts dafür geht.
Fertig geworden sind wir mit dem Erscheinungsbild der Ruhrtriennale trotz langer Tage und Nächte trotzdem nicht. Das aber ganz bewusst:
Denn das Festival sollte der Frage nachgehen, inwiefern Kunst und Religiosität des Menschen den gleichen inneren Ursprung haben.
Wir entwickelten dafür ein Signet, das in Pinselstrichmanier ein R (für Ruhr) bzw. eine 3 (für Triennale) darstellt und bewusst *unfertig* wirkt –
so wie es unsere Auseinandersetzung mit Kunst und Religion letztlich immer ist. Auf Gebäuden und Medien stehen
Handschrift, Bewegungsunschärfe und Auflösung der Bilder für die Auseinandersetzung mit den Weltreligionen,
für viel Spaß am Design und wenig Feierabend.

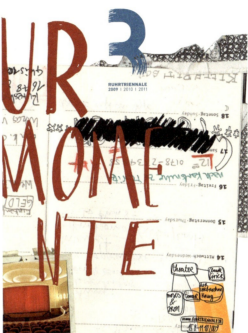

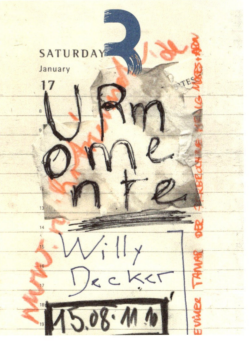

LITERAT

ROAD

RUHRTRIENNALE
2009 | 2010 | 2011

DEKALOG

EIN FILMZYKLUS VON KRZYSZTOF KIEŚLOWSKI
IM KINO CASABLANCA, BOCHUM

Eine Reihe der Ruhrtriennale

RUHRTRIENNALE
2009 | 2010 | 2011
URMOMENTE

DIE BLECHTROMMEL

RUHR
2009

URM

MOSES
UND ARON

ARNOLD SCHÖNBERG

RUHRTRIENNALE
2009 | 2010 | 2011
URMOMENTE

20.08. - 10.10.2010
WANDERUNG
SUCHE NACH DEM WEG

RUHRTRIENNALE
2009 | 2010 | 2011

Autland

WORK

2009 _ Emphasis on Judaism; graphic code > handwriting
2009 _ Schwerpunkt Judentum; grafische Chiffre > Handschrift

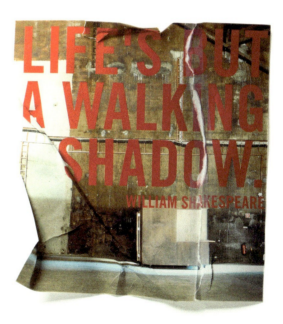

2011 _ Emphasis on Buddhism; graphic code > image decomposition
2011 _ Schwerpunkt Buddhismus; grafische Chiffre > Darstellung der Realität als reines Abbild

WORK

2010 _ emphasis on Islam; graphic code > motion blur
2010 _ Schwerpunkt Islam; grafische Chiffre > Bewegung

RUHRTRIENNALE
2009 | 2010 | 2011

momente

des Landkreises B

Allgemeinen Ortsk kasse

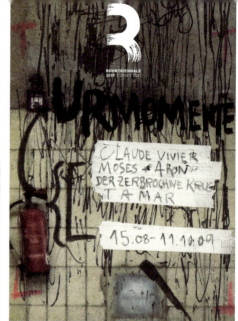

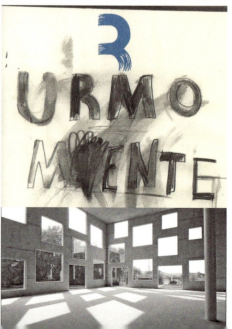

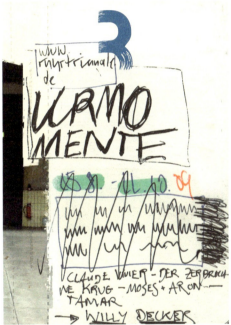

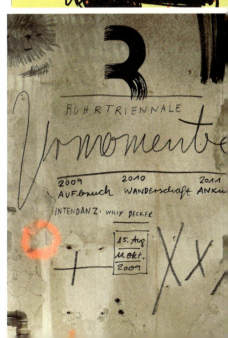

RUHRTRIENNALE
2009 | 2010 | 2011

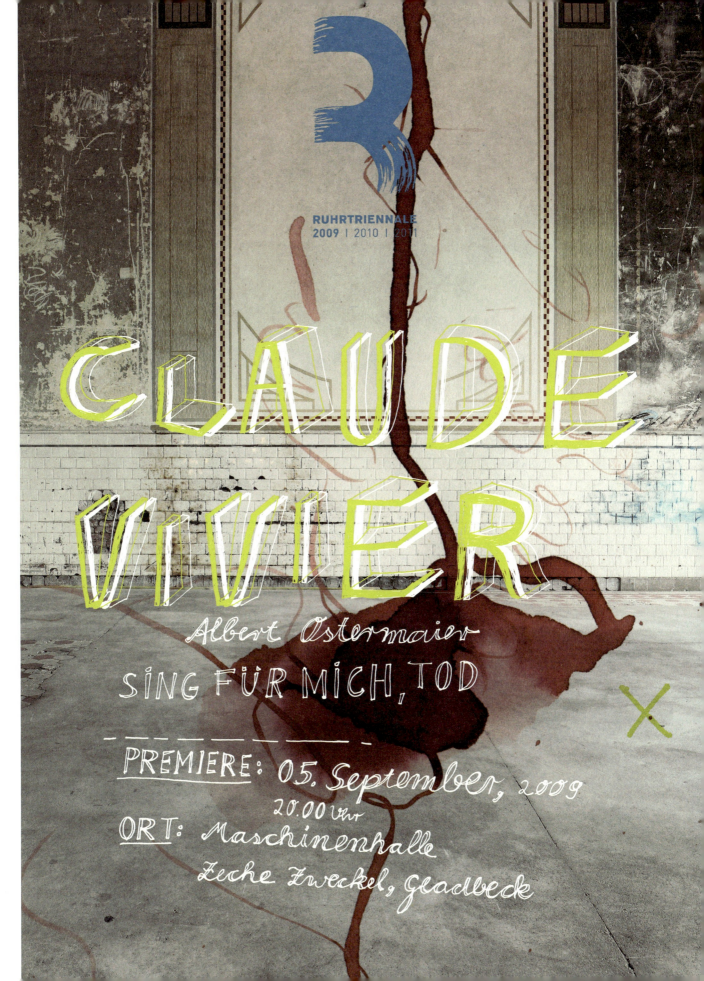

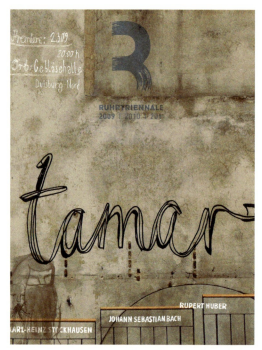

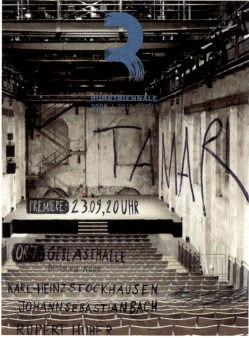

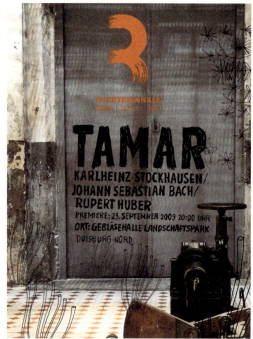

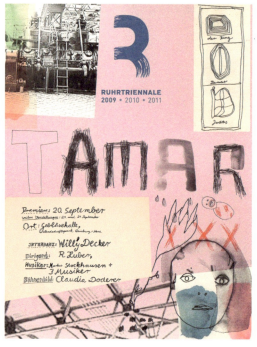

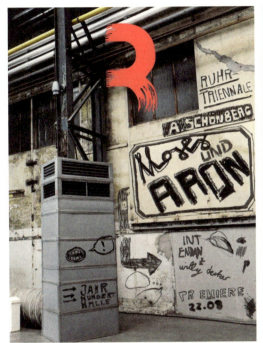

We designed 60 different illuminated posters for the _primal moments_ (Urmomente) theme as well as for the main performances.

Wir gestalteten 60 Citylightplakate für das Festivalmotto _Urmomente_ und die Hauptaufführungen.

2.0 /

GOOD DESIGN IS A TOUGH JOB.

.02

Good designers are never satisfied. Forever searching, forever at square one. Good design thrives on constantly failing without ever giving up. Good design is a creative process – without a rest on the seventh day.
Failing a hundred times to succeed once. The challenge and the reward are yours alone: design is what you live for. Your best project will always be your next one.

Gute Designer sind unzufrieden. Ständig auf der Suche, ständig am Anfang. Gutes Design lebt davon, beständig zu scheitern und niemals aufzugeben. Gutes Design ist ein schöpferischer Prozess – nur ohne die Ruhe am siebten Tag. Ist hundert Mal Versagen für ein Mal Erfolg. Anspruch und Lohn liegen nur in dir: Design ist Dasein.
Immer erst dein nächstes Projekt ist dein Bestes.

2.1 /

Corporate Design
CLIENT _ NATURENERGIEPLUS

(2011)

GREEN
ENERGY

Good design for a sensible product like green electricity – there is nothing better! There were immediately a hundred ideas; a little later a hundred designs; after that, hundreds of feelings of dissatisfaction. You say to yourself, »*There must be a better way!*« have a rethink, and continue honing and simplifying things. Then, finally, you find the perfect solution. The client is happy. Then, just when you think you can sit back and relax, the phone rings: »*We think your logo is really good. That's why we have a virtually identical one for our company.*« That can happen when there are more than eight million protected logos around the world. The simpler, clearer and more reduced a design is, the more likely it is to happen. There is no malicious intent or attempt to steal ideas; it's quite simply a case of bad luck. Good design is a tough job. So, back to the drawing board – sometimes it's the hundred thousandth design that ultimately achieves the breakthrough.

Gutes Design für ein sinnvolles Produkt wie Ökostrom – nichts lieber als das! Sofort waren hundert Ideen da, wenig später hundert Entwürfe, und hundertmal sagst du dir »*Da geht noch was!*«, denkst neu, schärfst und reduzierst weiter. Endlich: Die perfekte Lösung. Du und der Kunde im Glück. Und gerade, als du dich entspannt zurücklehnen möchtest, kommt ein Anruf: »*Ihr Signet ist wirklich prima, finden wir. Unsere Firma hat nämlich ein ganz ähnliches.*« So etwas kommt schon mal vor bei über acht Millionen geschützter Bildmarken weltweit – umso eher, je einfacher, klarer und reduzierter ein Entwurf ist. Klar, dass dabei kein Ideenklau, sondern ganz einfach nur Pech im Spiel ist: Good Design is a tough job. Also: Auf ein Neues – manchmal führt eben erst der hundertunderste Entwurf zum Ziel.

WORK

Above _ The final logo.
Oben _ Das finale Logo.

This page _ The initial look.
Auf dieser Seite _ Der ursprüngliche Auftritt.

3.0 /

GOOD DESIGN SPEAKS FOR ITSELF.

.03

Ingenious ideas are simple. As a matter of principle. Design either looks good or it doesn't, it works or it doesn't, it is exciting or it isn't: mere moments are crucial. Complexity gets you nowhere. If a design project needs explaining, the designer has failed.

Geniale Ideen sind einfach. Und zwar aus Prinzip.
Design sieht gut aus oder nicht, funktioniert oder nicht, ist spannend oder nicht:
Augenblicke entscheiden. Mit Komplexität ist nichts gewonnen.
Braucht ein Designprojekt Erklärungen, hat der Designer versagt.
Design, das nicht von selbst wirkt, ist ein hübscher Versuch, aber kein Ergebnis.

3.1 /

Design
CLIENT _ BFF

(2009 – 2011)

TAKE A
LOOK...

What do you do when you are asked by the best German photographers to design their annual?
You think about photos. Since the book depicts the *who, where and what*, we wanted the design to address the *how*.
Using a partially transparent slipcase and punched holes, we turned the 2009 annual into a fully functional camera obscura.
The following year we simulated a rangefinder camera, and in 2011 we honoured the display of a single-lens
reflex camera – thanks to lenticular film, the BFF logo can be focused by rotating the book.

Was machst du, wenn du von den besten deutschen Fotografen gebeten wirst, ihren Jahresband zu gestalten?
Du denkst über Fotos nach. Weil das Buch *wer, wo und was* zeigt, wollten wir in der Gestaltung dem *wie* nachgehen –
und machten das Jahrbuch 2009 mithilfe eines teiltransparenten Schubers und Lochstanzung zur voll funktionsfähigen Camera Obscura.
Im Folgejahr simulierten wir eine Sucherkamera und setzten 2011 dem Display einer Spiegelreflexkamera ein Denkmal –
dank Lentikularfolie kann man durch Drehen des Buches das BFF-Logo scharf stellen.

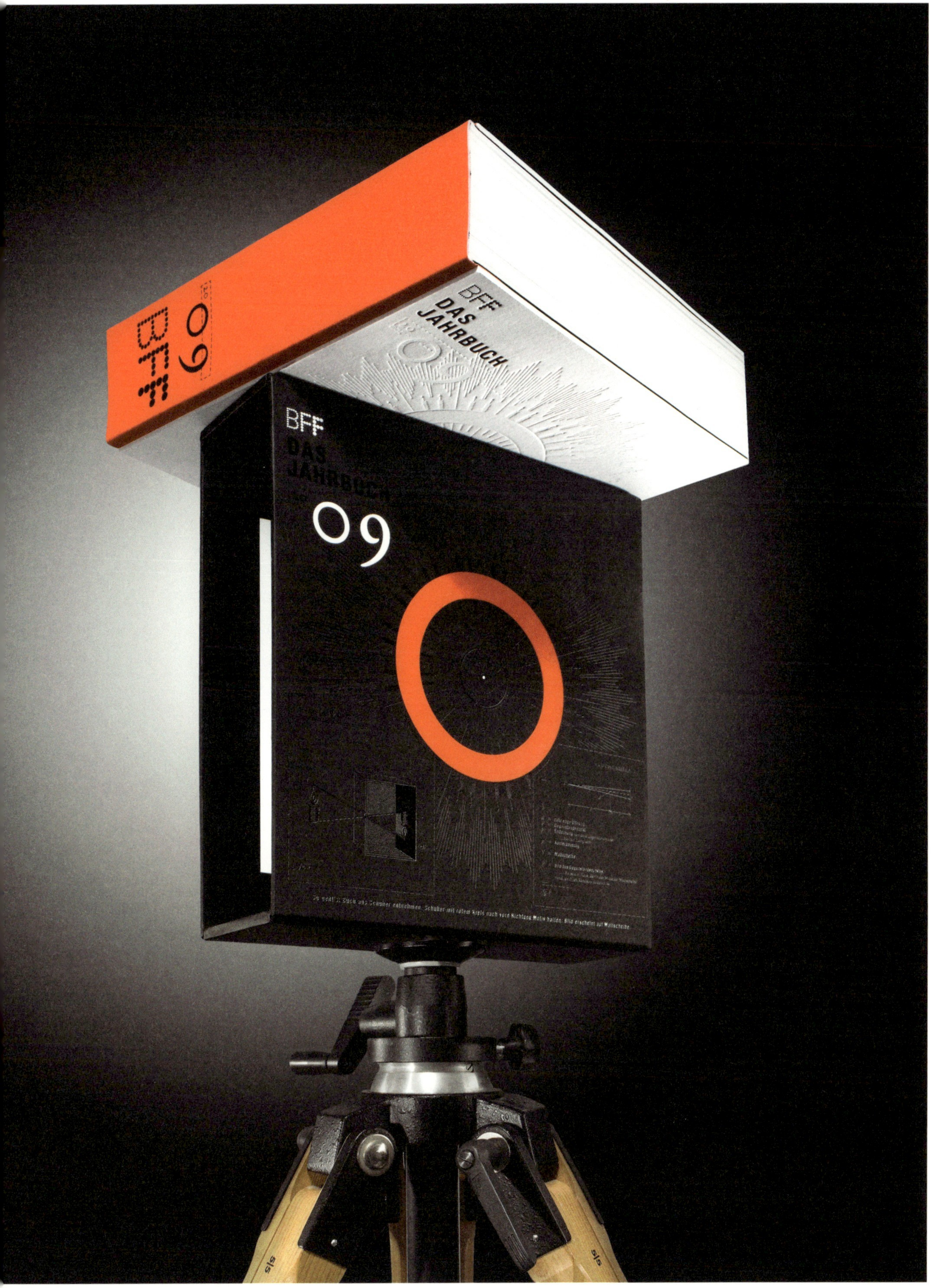
BFF
09
BFF
DAS
JAHRBUCH
BFF
DAS
JAHRBUCH
09

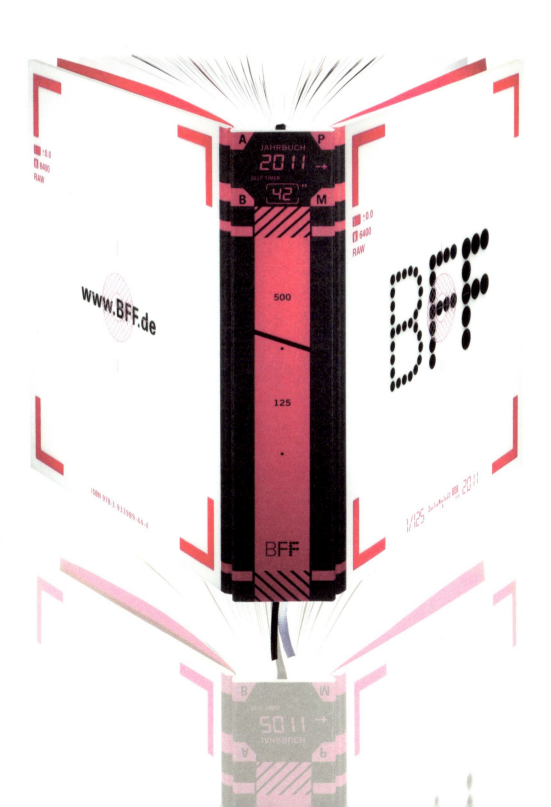

3.2 /

Packaging
CLIENT _ STRICHPUNKT

(2000)

READY FOR CHRISTMAS:
CUT.

With many clients, the relationships built up over the years verge on the familial – when it comes down to it, you sometimes see your clients more often than you see your partner. So what could be more fitting than inviting the clients to a traditional German Christmas dinner: ROAST GOOSE. Since the table in our living room would not have been quite big enough, we sent utensils as gifts so that the by-products could be put to good use – from poultry scissors to an ink pot for the goose quill, and a pillowcase as a useful way of storing all that down. Everything came with self-explanatory pictographs so that nothing could go wrong amidst all the typical Christmas chaos – at the end of the day, we didn't want to be responsible for any family rows over the festive period. By way of a thank you, in January we received a little jar of goose fat from two clients.

Mit vielen Kunden entstehen über die Jahre nahezu familiäre Beziehungen – schließlich sieht man seinen Kunden teils öfter als seinen Partner. Was lag also näher, als die Auftraggeber auch zum traditionellen deutschen Weihnachtsessen einzuladen: zum Gänsebraten. Weil der Tisch in unserem Wohnzimmer nicht ganz ausgereicht hätte, verschenkten wir Utensilien zum guten Gelingen und zur Verwertung der Nebenprodukte – von der Geflügelschere über ein Tuschefässchen für den Gänsekiel bis hin zur Kissenhülle, um die Daunen sinnstiftend unterzubringen. Alles mit selbsterklärenden Piktogrammen ausgestattet, damit in der typischen Weihnachtshektik nichts schiefgehen kann – schließlich wollten wir am Familienstreit nicht auch noch an den Feiertagen schuld sein. Als Dank bekamen wir im Januar gleich von zwei Adressaten ein Gläschen Gänseschmalz.

3.3 /

Packaging
CLIENT _ VERLAG HERMANN SCHMIDT MAINZ

(2004)

MADE TO MEASURE _
DTP

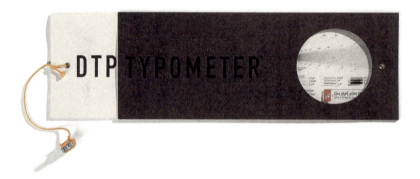

No designer's desk has been complete over the past few decades without a typographic ruler. This has all changed in the age of the DTP, but it still doesn't take anything away from its usefulness when it comes to determining font sizes. That is just what the VERLAG HERMANN SCHMIDT MAINZ thought, so it developed a DTP typographic ruler using a highly elaborate silk-screen and calibration process. The result was hardly cheap, but it certainly looked it. We changed all that by hiding the plastic strip in suitably classy packaging with various embossing and refinements. We also dug deep into the typographic vault and attached a D, T, and P in hot type on every typographic ruler – nicely bound, of course.

Ein Typometer war vom Designerschreibtisch vergangener Jahrzehnte nicht wegzudenken – ganz anders im DTP-Zeitalter, was nichts an seiner Nützlichkeit bei der Bestimmung von Schriftgrößen ändert. Das dachte sich auch der Verlag Hermann Schmidt Mainz und entwickelte ein DTP-Typometer in einem höchst aufwändigen Siebdruck- und Eichverfahren. Das Ergebnis war eine nicht ganz billige Angelegenheit, sah aber nicht unbedingt danach aus. Das änderten wir, indem wir den Plastikstreifen in eine würdige Verpackung mit diversen Prägungen und Veredelungen steckten. Zusätzlich griffen wir tief in die typografische Mottenkiste und hängten an jedes Typometer ein D, T und P in Form von Bleisatzlettern an – sauber abgebunden, versteht sich.

Embossed elements in the packaging.

Tiefprägung auf der Umverpackung.

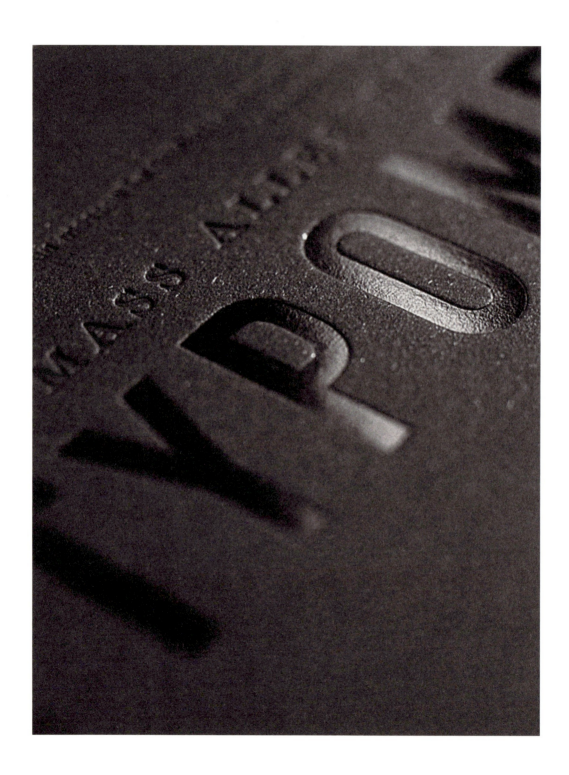

Successful anachronism: DTP in hot type.

Ein erfolgreicher Widerspruch in sich: DTP als Bleisatz.

3.3 /

Annual Report
CLIENT _ DAIMLER

(2008)

VALUES BY THE
LETTER

Expressing the most important values of a newly set-up corporation is an intricate matter – in most cases a bunch of management consultants are worn down, twenty workshops are held, and at the end of it all the outcome is always the same. At Daimler it all happened rather more quickly following its divestment from CHRYSLER. We came up with the solution after a couple of hours of deliberation, and it took the management board less than 20 minutes to approve it: we simply assigned seven attributes to the new corporation name DAIMLER – one for each letter. The result was a set of guiding principles consisting of Dedication, Ambition, Innovation, Mobility, Leadership, Efficiency and Responsibility. To signal that the management stood behind the brand, we quite simply positioned them behind it. A board member then promptly bought one of the metal letters – as a birthday present for his wife, whose name began with the same letter.

Die wichtigsten Werte eines neu aufgestellten Konzerns zu formulieren, ist eine verzwickte Sache – meist werden dafür ein Rudel Unternehmensberater verschlissen, zwanzig Workshops durchgeführt und am Ende kommt bei allen das Gleiche heraus. Bei Daimler ging das nach der Trennung von Chrysler etwas schneller – die Lösung hatten wir nach ein paar Stunden Nachdenken und die Verabschiedung im Vorstand dauerte nicht mal zwanzig Minuten: Wir ordneten ganz einfach dem neuen Konzernnamen Daimler sieben Attribute zu – eines für jeden Buchstaben. So wurde aus Dedication, Ambition, Innovation, Mobility, Leadership, Efficiency und Responsibility das neue Leitbild. Um zu signalisieren, dass die Führung hinter der Marke steht, stellten wir sie ebenso einfach – dahinter. Einen der Blechbuchstaben kaufte danach prompt ein Vorstandsmitglied – als Geburtstagsgeschenk für seine Frau, deren Vorname damit anfängt.

DAIMLER

DAIMLER

Geschäftsbericht 2007

Mitglieder des Vorstands

The six-foot-eight-inch-tall Daimler CEO Dr Dieter Zetsche in front of a five-foot "D" – the letters for the complete board were a bit smaller in size.

Zweimetermann und Daimler-Chef Dr. Dieter Zetsche vor einem 1,50 m hohen „D" – die Buchstaben für den Gesamtvorstand waren etwas kleiner.

DAIMLER

ded|i|ca|tion [Hingabe, die] <*lat.*>; Die Leidenschaft für immer bessere Produkte und höchste Qualität treibt uns an. Sie ist die Basis für unsere führende Position im Wettbewerb. Wir wollen unsere Kunden mit **faszinierenden Premium-Pkw, erstklassigen Nutzfahrzeugen** und **maßgeschneiderten Serviceleistungen** begeistern. Und das immer wieder neu.

10

A

I

am|bi|tion [Anspruch, der] <*lat.*>; Als Pionier des Automobilbaus wollen wir auch die Zukunft der Mobilität nachhaltig gestalten. Gerade als Premium-Hersteller haben wir den Anspruch, mit **richtungsweisenden Produkten, Technologien** und **Ideen** Maßstäbe zu setzen.

in|no|va|tion [Innovation, die] <*lat.*>; Innovation hat bei Daimler Tradition: Die Namen Gottlieb Daimler, Karl Benz und Wilhelm Maybach sind untrennbar mit der Entwicklung des Automobils verbunden. Zahlreiche Innovationen stammen aus unserem Haus. Und die Liebe zum **Erfinden** ist auch heute unser **wichtigstes Kapital.**

M

mo|bi|li|ty [Mobilität, die] <lat.>; Wer etwas bewegen möchte, muss selbst beweglich sein. Seit 120 Jahren prägen wir die Entwicklung der Mobilität und haben uns dabei immer wieder selbst neu erfunden. Wir stellen uns auch in Zukunft der Verantwortung, Mobilität sicher und sauber zu gestalten – und wir bleiben entsprechend dynamisch.

L

lead|er|ship [Führung, die] <techn.>; Wir haben uns einer Kultur der Spitzenleistung verpflichtet: Wir möchten unsere Kunden mit herausragenden Produkten und Dienstleistungen begeistern, der Arbeitgeber der Wahl für die talentiertesten Köpfe sein und unsere Aktionäre durch unsere Ertragskraft überzeugen. Wir sind stolz auf unsere einzigartige Tradition und arbeiten mit Leidenschaft für eine erfolgreiche Zukunft.

E

ef|fi|cien|cy [Effizienz, die] <lat.>; Effizienz ist eine unverzichtbare Grundlage für unseren wirtschaftlichen Erfolg und dauerhaft profitables Wachstum. Wir messen uns konsequent mit den Besten der Branche und streben nach kontinuierlicher Effizienzsteigerung — nicht nur bei unserer täglichen Arbeit, sondern auch im Umgang mit den natürlichen Ressourcen.

R

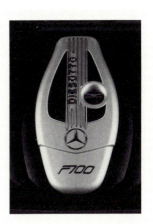

re|spon|si|bi|li|ty [Verantwortung, die] <lat.>; Als globales Unternehmen wissen wir um unsere Mitverantwortung für die gesellschaftliche Entwicklung. Eine tragfähige Balance von wirtschaftlichen, ökologischen und sozialen Ansprüchen ist der Maßstab unseres Handelns. Dabei stehen wir im offenen Dialog und orientieren uns an höchsten ethischen Grundsätzen. So schaffen wir bleibende Werte.

4.0 /

GOOD DESIGN IS TIME- LESS.

.04

Good design harbours two units of time: one for its genesis and one for its impact.
The former is not a measure and the latter is immeasurable.
If the response to your efforts is 'Not bad for the time available', throw it away. If the reaction is 'A child of its time', use it for advertising.
Good design defies time. It works for the moment without burning itself out. It appears fresh again and again – no matter when or how quickly it was conceived.

Gutes Design birgt zwei Zeiteinheiten: Die seiner Entstehung und die seiner Wirkung.
Die erste ist kein Maßstab, die zweite nicht messbar. Wenn es über dein Ergebnis heißt:
„Für die verfügbare Zeit nicht schlecht": Schmeiß es weg. Wenn es darüber heißt:
„Ein Kind seiner Zeit": Mach Werbung daraus. Gutes Design schafft die Zeit ab.
Es wirkt im Augenblick, aber verbrennt sich nicht darin. Es wirkt auf Dauer neu – egal,
wie schnell und wann es entstand.

4.1 /

Corporate Design & e-books
CLIENT _ MYSKOOB

(2011)

CLASSICS OF THE
DIGITAL AGE

Opposites attract: such as the future of literature and its past. Classic texts as e-books: an interface between the two worlds; perfect for a timeless design approach. The start-up company originally wanted to produce a kind of photostory. We felt that was too fashionable and agreed upon a more typographically oriented concept. To ensure that the classics were able to make the transition to the new media world in a befitting manner, we broke from traditional book design: it wasn't the title of the book that appeared in big letters on the first page, but the name of the hero. Just like on the Web, everyone is on first-name terms with everyone else, and the bookshelf in the iBookstore is simply a great deal smaller than the one in the bookshop around the corner.

Gegensätze ziehen sich an: Zum Beispiel die Zukunft der Literatur und ihre Vergangenheit. Klassische Texte in e-Books: Eine Schnittstelle zwischen den Welten, wie gemacht für einen zeitlosen Gestaltungsansatz. Ursprünglich wollte das Start-up-Unternehmen eine Art Fotoroman inszenieren. Das empfanden wir als zu modisch und einigten uns auf ein stärker typographisch geprägtes Konzept. Damit die Klassiker den Transfer in die neue Medienwelt angemessen vollziehen können, haben wir dabei mit der herkömmlichen Buchgestaltung gebrochen: Auf der Startseite ist nicht der Titel des Werks groß zu sehen, sondern der Name des Helden. Ganz wie im Web: Jeder ist mit jedem gleich per Du, und das Buchregal im iBooks-Store ist einfach deutlich kleiner als das im Buchladen um die Ecke.

Books become MySkoob: Classic literature, but a little different. The logo is reminiscent of a bookmark.
Aus Books wird MySkoob: Klassische Literatur einmal anders. Das Signet erinnert an ein Lesezeichen.

MY/SKOOB

GET PASSI ON ATE ! WE ♥ STORIES

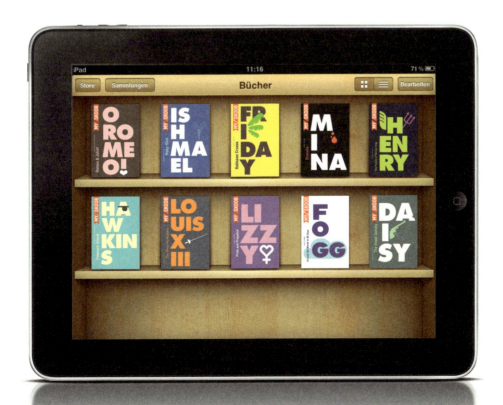

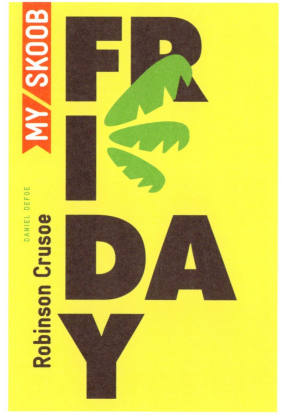

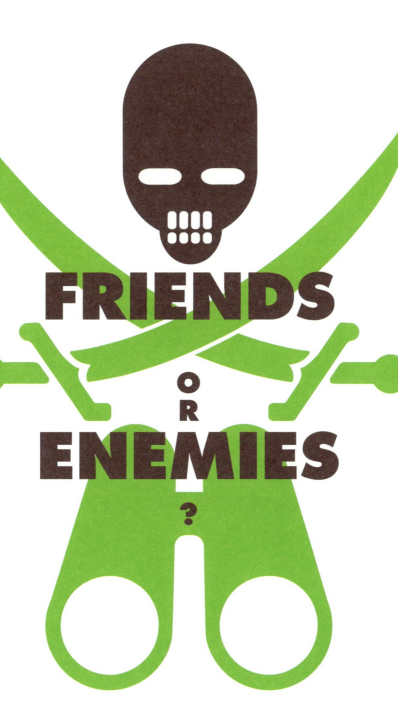

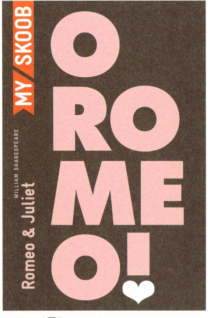

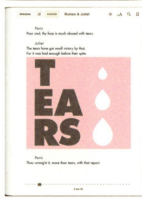

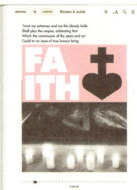

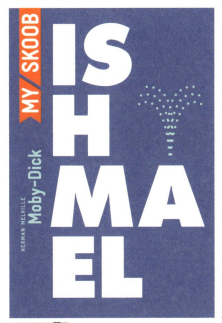

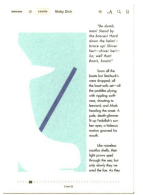

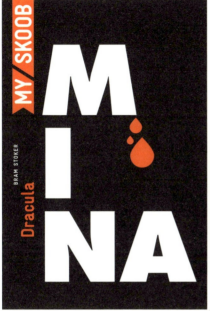

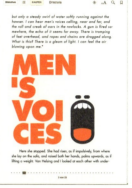

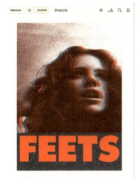

4.2 /

Corporate Design & Annual Report

CLIENT _ 4MBO INTERNATIONAL ELECTRONIC AG

(2002)

/ THE WORK OF _ STRICHPUNKT /

PERFECT FOR THE

MARKET

A chart says more than a thousand words: for the complex business of the electronics supplier 4MBO we didn't say anything big. To be precise, we didn't say anything at all. That is because everything the company has to say, it says with striking, minimal infographics – whether they relate to the market share for blood pressure monitors, the potential of the laptop business or foreign turnover. We designed it all so timelessly that it was published many times in design annuals – and one year later we found our graphics reproduced one-to-one in the dissertation of a job applicant. Incidentally, the title of the dissertation was *Early Bird*.

Ein Chart sagt mehr als tausend Worte: Für das komplexe Geschäft des Elektronikanbieters 4MBO haben wir keine großen Worte gemacht. Genau genommen gar keine. Denn alles, was das Unternehmen zu sagen hat, tut es anhand plakativer, reduzierter Infografiken – ob es nun um den Marktanteil bei Blutdruckmessgeräten, die Potenziale des Laptop-Geschäfts oder den Auslandsumsatz geht. Das Ganze gestalteten wir so zeitlos, dass es vielfach in Designjahrbüchern abgedruckt wurde – und wir unsere Grafiken prompt ein Jahr später eins zu eins in der Diplomarbeit eines Bewerbers wiederfanden. Der Titel der Diplomarbeit übrigens: *Early Bird*.

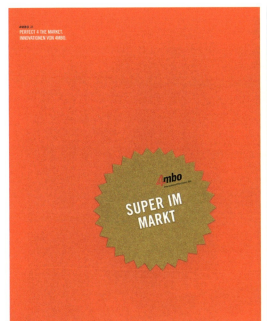

Nothing is more ephemeral than current electronic products. That is why we didn't even illustrate them, but rather scanned them from adverts with an extra-large grid; but not without endowing the reverse side in gold and crimson with the finest typography in order to emphasise the quality of the products in a befitting manner.

Nichts ist vergänglicher als aktuelle Elektronikprodukte. Weshalb wir diese, wo es nötig war, gar nicht erst abgebildet, sondern aus Anzeigen mit extragroßem Raster herausgescannt haben – aber nicht, ohne die Rückseite in Gold und Purpur mit feinster Typo zu versehen, um den Wert der Geräte gebührend herauszustellen.

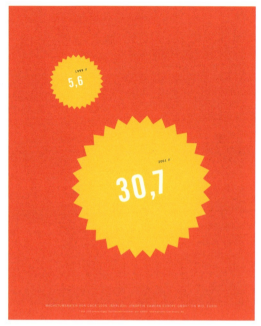

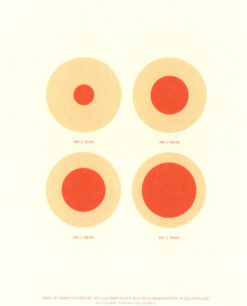

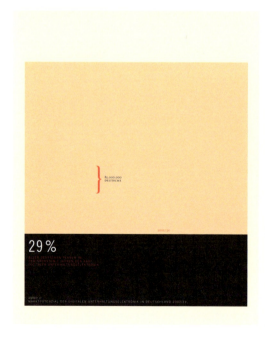

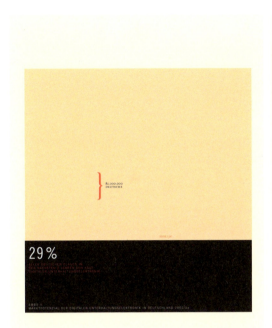

29 %

283,9

195,5

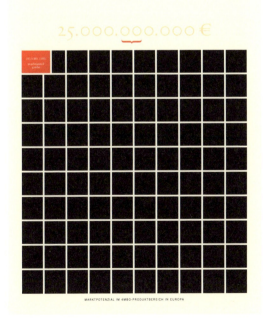

25.000.000.000 €

MARKTPOTENZIAL IM 4MBO-PRODUKTBEREICH IN EUROPA

1999 = 7 %   AUSLANDSUMSATZ 4MBO-KONZERN   2001 = 23,6 %

WORK

4.3 /

Corporate Design
CLIENT _ KLANGERFINDER

(2010)

/ THE WORK OF _ STRICHPUNKT /

SOUND
DESIGN

The Art Directors Club is mostly overrun with advertisers *(see also chapter 17)*. Designers and composers have always been the rather more exotic members – so it's no wonder that we made friends at the conventions and were ultimately given the privilege of coming up with a new corporate design for KLANGERFINDER. A challenge for us, because there aren't that many graphic options when it comes to sounds. Instead of notes we designed sound images that keep reinventing themselves using generative design parameters, thus remaining timeless. Consequently, oscillograms and rhythmic form sequences are the basis of the corporate design.

Im Art Directors Club tummeln sich vor allem Werber *(siehe auch Kap. 17)*. Designer und Komponisten waren unter den Mitgliedern eher Exoten – kein Wunder, dass wir uns bei den Treffen angefreundet haben und schließlich für die KLANGERFINDER ein Corporate Design erfinden durften. Eine Herausforderung für uns, weil es nur wenige grafische Umsetzungsmöglichkeiten für Töne gibt. Statt Noten haben wir Klang-Bilder entwickelt, die sich über generative Gestaltungsparameter immer wieder neu erfinden und dadurch zeitlos bleiben: Oszillogramme und rhythmische Formabfolgen werden so zu den Grundlagen des Corporate Designs.

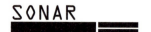

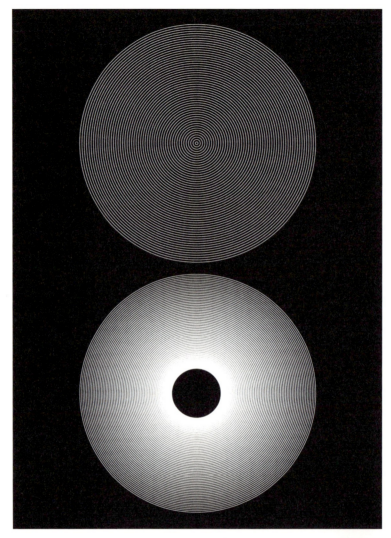

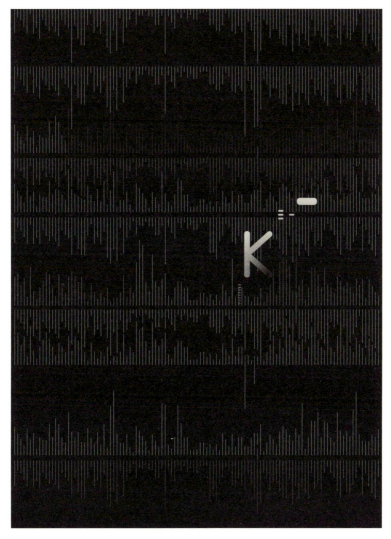

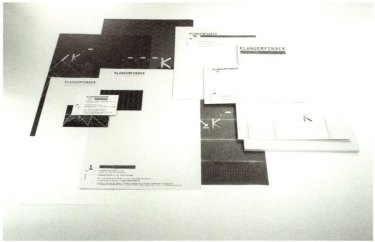

WORK

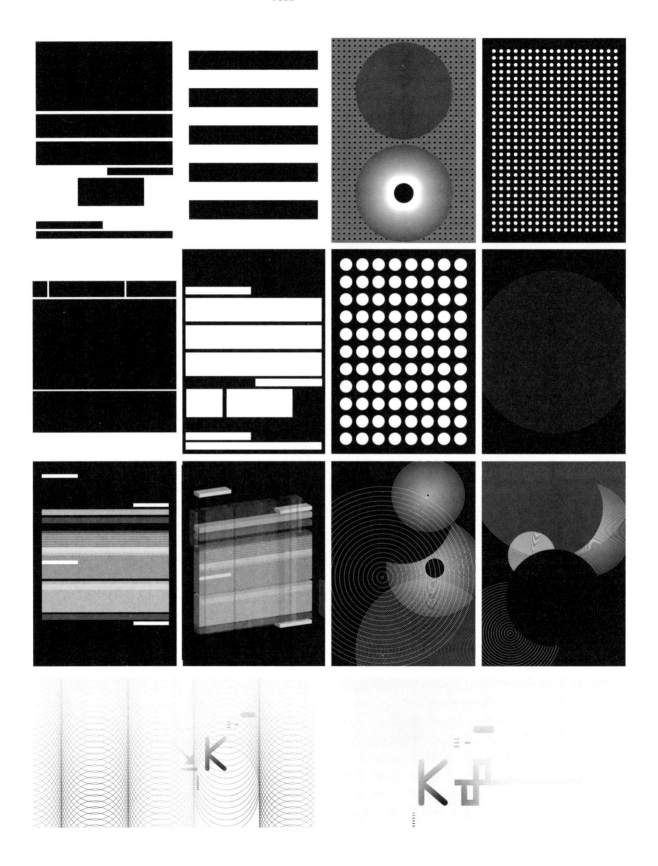

THESIS

5.0 /

GOOD DESIGN IS SLOW.

.05

Don't trust anyone who tells you creativity can be learnt.
It is something inside you.
Whether you use it for dollars, dignity, design or not at all is your decision.
Even if someone is an expert at InDesign or Ikebana, it doesn't make them a designer.
Good design is more than skilled craftsmanship – it is a good idea that takes time to mature.
The best design school is having time to call one's own.

Traue keinem, der dir sagt, dass du Kreativität lernen kannst. Sie ist in dir.
Ob du sie für Geld, Geltung, Gestaltung oder gar nicht nutzt, ist deine Sache.
Wer InDesign oder Ikebana perfekt beherrscht, ist noch lange kein Gestalter.
Gute Gestaltung ist mehr als gutes Handwerk, es ist ein guter Gedanke,
der Zeit braucht, um zu wachsen. Die beste Designschule ist Zeit für sich selbst.

5.1 /

Corporate Design
CLIENT _ STATE THEATRE STUTTGART

(2005)

THREE IN
ONE

The Stuttgart-based STATE THEATRE – the largest of its kind in Europe, employing over 1,200 people in three sections covering opera, ballet and theatre – invited 12 agencies to present their ideas for its new corporate design. Eleven of them presented sketches of logos to the panel of artistic directors. We came solely with questions – and were awarded the contract. It quickly became clear not only to us that a lasting corporate design requires time for a profound discussion – even more so in an institution with completely different spheres of activity. At the next meeting we had to wait for two hours in the opera dressing room following our presentation – the artistic directors had been arguing intensely about the initial designs. In the end it took two years before everyone could agree upon a uniform standard for the shared visual identity – with plenty of freedom for each individual section.

Zwölf Agenturen hatten die WÜRTTEMBERGISCHEN STAATSTHEATER, das größte Dreispartenhaus Europas mit über 1.200 Angestellten für Oper, Ballett und Schauspiel, zur Vorstellung ihrer Ideen für ein neues Corporate Design eingeladen. Elf davon präsentierten der Intendantenrunde Logoentwürfe. Wir kamen nur mit Fragen – und bekamen den Auftrag. Nicht nur uns war schnell klar geworden, dass ein nachhaltiges Corporate Design viel Zeit für eine tiefgreifende Auseinandersetzung benötigt – erst recht in einem Haus mit ganz unterschiedlichen Betätigungsfeldern. Beim nächsten Treffen mussten wir nach unserer Präsentation erst mal zwei Stunden in der Operngarderobe warten – die Intendanten hatten sich über die ersten Entwürfe kräftig in die Wolle gekriegt. Schließlich brauchte es volle zwei Jahre, bis man sich auf einheitliche Standards des gemeinsamen Auftritts einigen konnte – mit ausreichenden Freiräumen für jede einzelne Sparte.

STAATSOPERSTUTTGART   STUTTGARTER**BALLETT**   **SCHAUSPIEL**STUTTGART

staatstheaterstuttgart °

The Staatstheater Stuttgart publishes more than 10,000 printed pages every year – plus a website, banners, posters, signs and promotional merchandise. To cope with it all, we introduced strict typographic guidelines using the Compatil font, developed a colour coding system for the three sections and reduced the specified size for booklets from 17 to three. Most important of all, however, were the premiere tickets offered to our team as compensation for all the overtime we put in.

Das Staatstheater Stuttgart publiziert mehr als 10.000 Printseiten pro Jahr – dazu kommen Website, Fassadenbespielung, Plakate, Wegweisung und Werbeartikel. Um der Menge Herr zu werden, führten wir mit der Compatil eine einheitliche Hausschrift ein, entwickelten ein Farbsystem für die drei Sparten und reduzierten die Formate für Broschüren von 17 auf drei. Die wichtigste Maßnahme war allerdings, unserem Team Premierenkarten als Überstundenausgleich anzubieten.

6.0 /

GOOD DESIGN IS UN- COMFORT- ABLE.

.06

Artwork that appeals to everyone is ineffective and boring. Design needs edges, corners, imperfections, provocations and breaking points. Antagonism experienced by creator and user. Only then does design come to life. Classic designs are fine for upper-class retirement homes and executive villas; they move nothing and no one. So get going: only new ideas count!

Gestaltung, die allen gut gefällt, ist wirkungslos und langweilig.
Design braucht Ecken, Kanten, Unfertiges, Unbequemes, Sollbruchstellen.
Widerstand beim Macher und beim Nutzer. Nur dann ist Design lebendig.
Designklassiker sind gut für Schickeria-Altenheime und Vorstandsdatschen,
sie bewegen nichts und niemanden. Rührt euch: Nur das Neue zählt!

6.1 /

Corporate Design
CLIENT _ STUTTGART STATE OPERA

(2006 – 2008)

/ THE WORK OF _ STRICHPUNKT /

DESIGNING IS JUST AN
ACT

Good design can be pretty uncomfortable – if it becomes too successful, for example. As was the case with the design of the visual identity for the STAATSOPER STUTTGART. Initially, there was a good mood surrounding the design of the logo: since the opera house was built on the former site of the royal botanical gardens, we designed a rosette as a logo and composed motifs from the wholesale flower market to go with it for the first season. The drama took its course with the design of the programmes: whilst the first productions came in for harsh criticism, the programmes were very well received. When the local press eventually advised the opera to align the quality onstage with the quality of the programmes, the time had come to end the collaboration. A conciliatory conclusion: at the end of the directorship we were nonetheless given the task of designing the book on the subject of five years of the STAATSOPER STUTTGART.

Gutes Design kann ganz schön unbequem sein – zum Beispiel dann, wenn es zu erfolgreich wird. Wie bei der Gestaltung des Auftritts für die Staatsoper Stuttgart. Freude herrschte noch bei der Entwicklung des Signets: Weil das Opernhaus auf dem ehedem königlichen botanischen Garten gebaut wurde, entwickelten wir als Logo eine Rosette und komponierten für die erste Spielzeit Motive aus dem Blumengroßmarkt dazu. Das Drama nahm mit der Gestaltung der Programmhefte seinen Lauf: Während sich die ersten Inszenierungen herbe Kritik gefallen lassen mussten, kamen die Hefte bestens an. Als schließlich die lokale Presse der Oper riet, die Qualität auf der Bühne der Qualität der Programme anzugleichen, war das das Ende der Zusammenarbeit. Versöhnlicher Abschluss: am Ende der Intendanz gestalteten wir dann doch das Buch über fünf Jahre Staatsoper Stuttgart.

STAATSOPERSTUTTGART
staatstheaterstuttgart

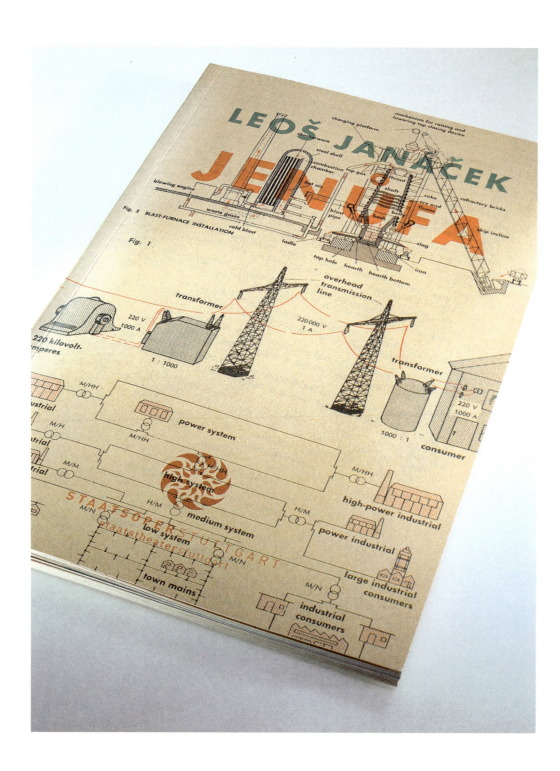

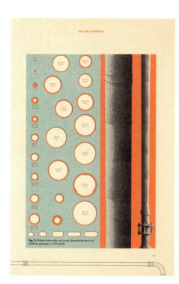

As part of the corporate design, we used to produce our very own interpretation of the stage action in a matter of days, combine it with photos from Friday's dress rehearsal and present a freshly printed programme for Sunday's premiere – from a twenties-style electronics catalogue for *Jenufa* (this page) and a Western libretto for *Il Fanciulla del West*, to a credit card satire for *Der Fliegende Holländer* and a criminal file for *Carmen*.

Innerhalb des CD-Rahmens visualisierten wir in jeweils nur wenigen Tagen unsere ganz eigenständigen Interpretationen des Bühnengeschehens, kombinierten diese freitags mit Fotos der Generalprobe und legten sonntags zur Premiere ein druckfrisches Programmheft vor – vom Elektrokatalog im Zwanziger-Jahre-Look für *Jenufa (diese Seite)* über ein Westernlibretto für *Il Fanciulla del West* bis zur Kreditkartenpersiflage beim *Fliegenden Holländer* und einer Kriminalakte für *Carmen*.

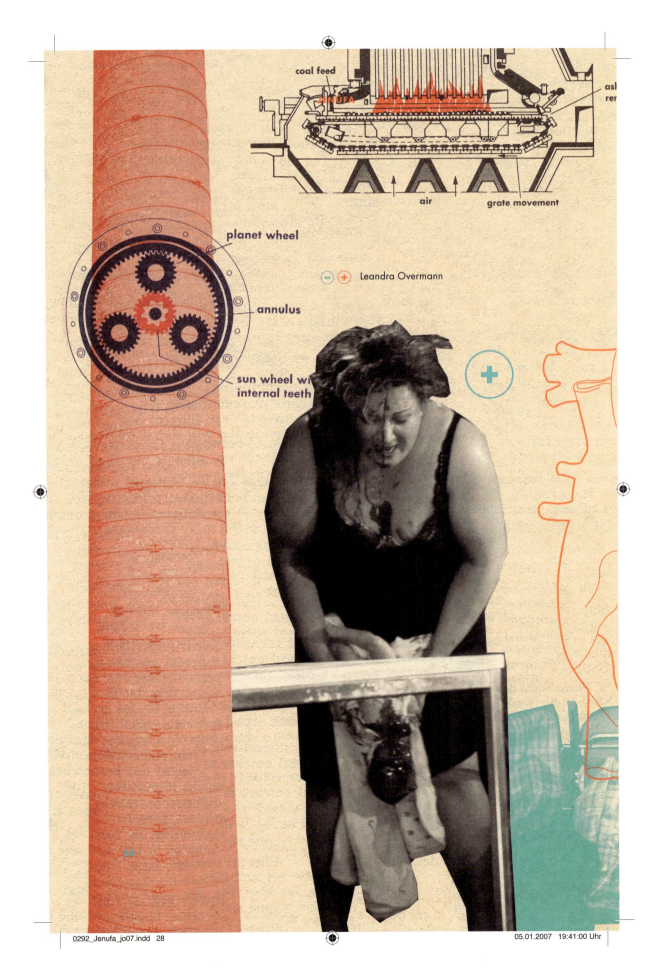

coal feed

ash
rem

air   grate movement

planet wheel

Leandra Overmann

annulus

sun wheel wi
internal teeth

ash
removal

roller guide
ring

ratchet

hub f
holes

a

b

Frank van Aken, Mark Munkittrick

29

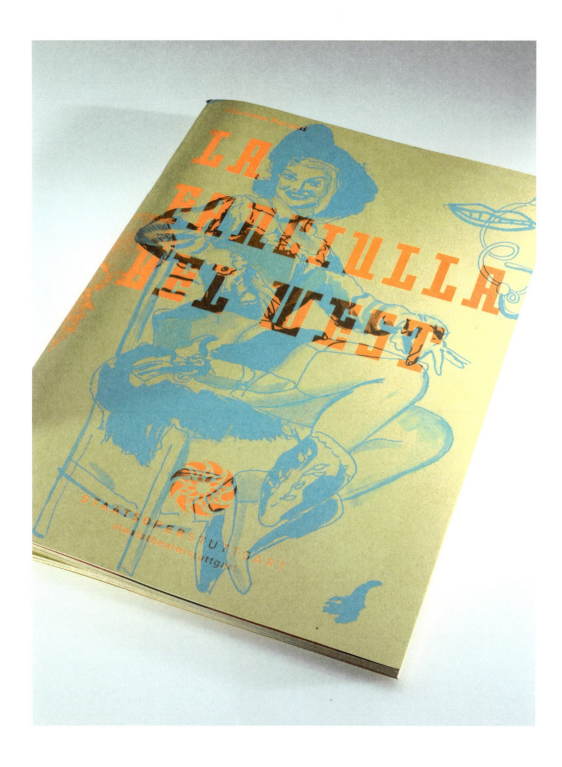

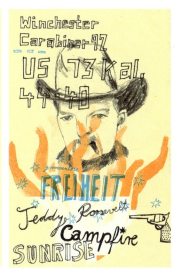

Giacomo Puccini: *La Fanciulla del West*

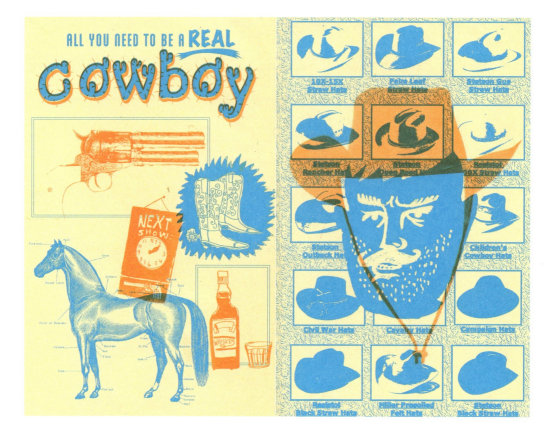

 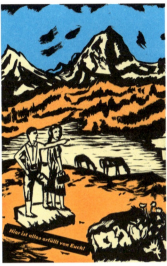 

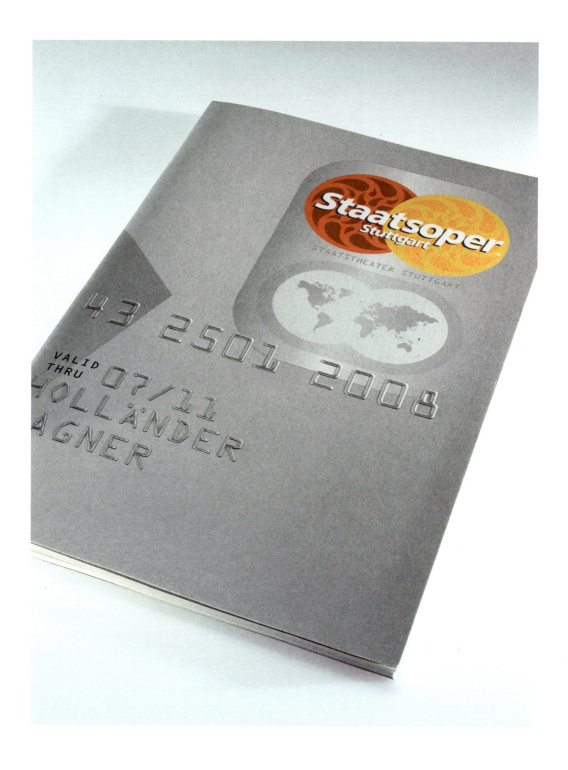

WORK

Richard Wagner: *Der fliegende Holländer*

Der fliegende Holländer   PREM.: 25012008   Urfassung 1841   01/2008
Staatsoper Stuttgart   19:30
                                             Kontoauszug   EUR-Konto

Bu-Tag Wert Vorgang   Belastungen Gutschriften

Der fliegende Holländer   PREM.: 25012008   Urfassung 1841   01/2008
Staatsoper Stuttgart   19:30
                                              K o n t o a u s z u g   EUR-Konto

Bu-Tag Wert Vorgang   Belastungen Gutschriften

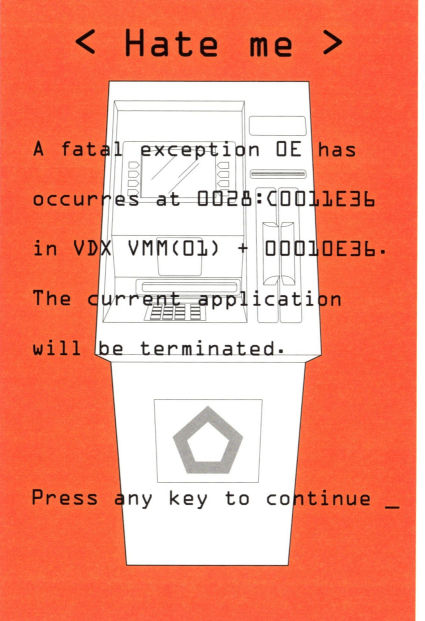

Press any key to continue _

1303

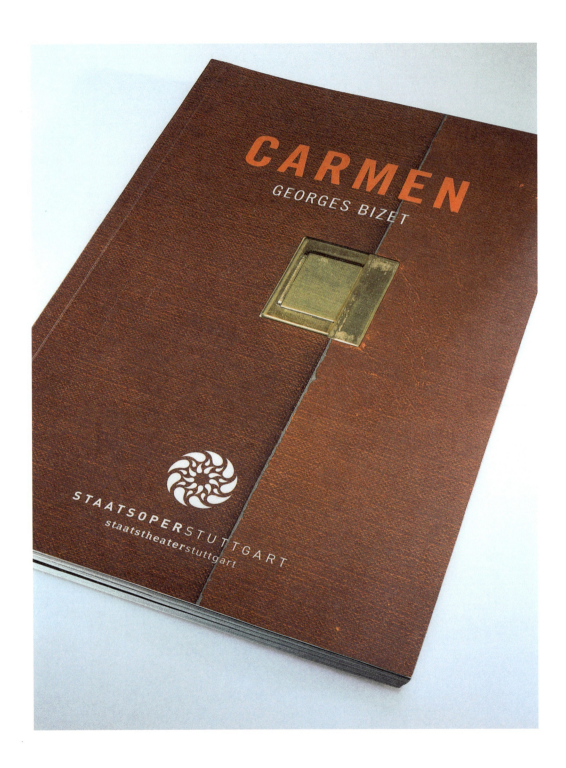

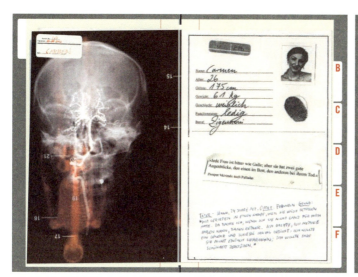

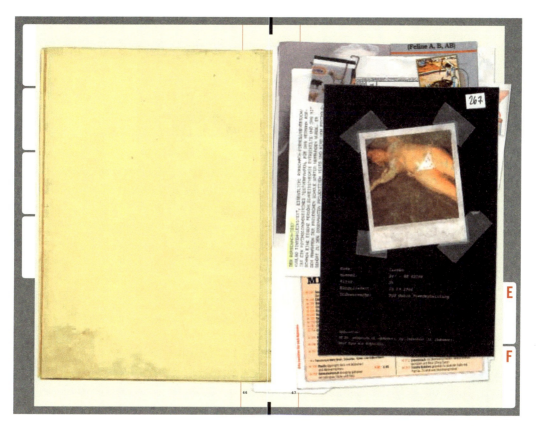

Georges Bizet: *Carmen*

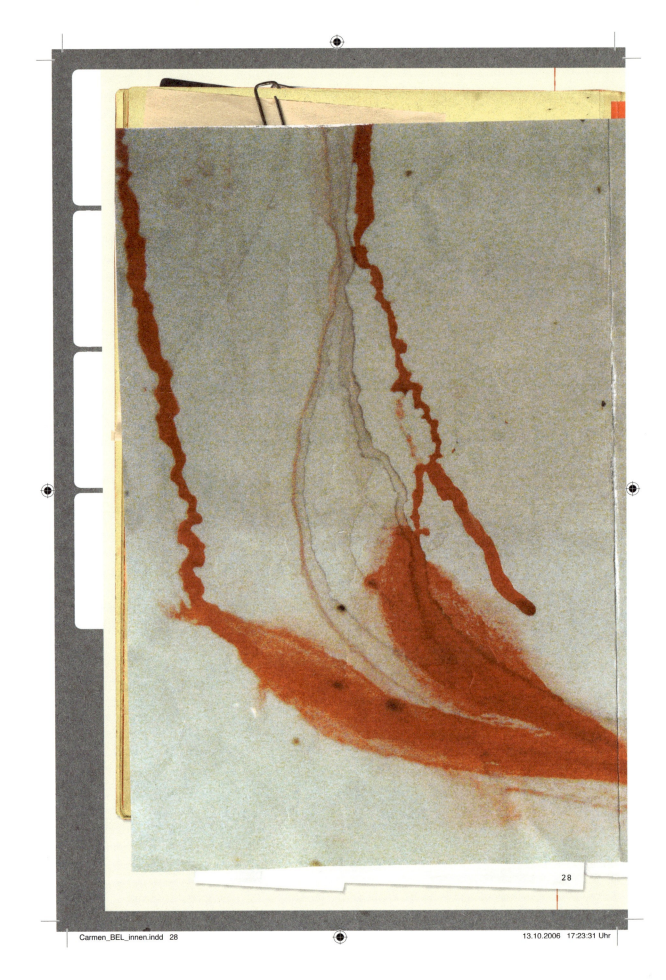

E

F

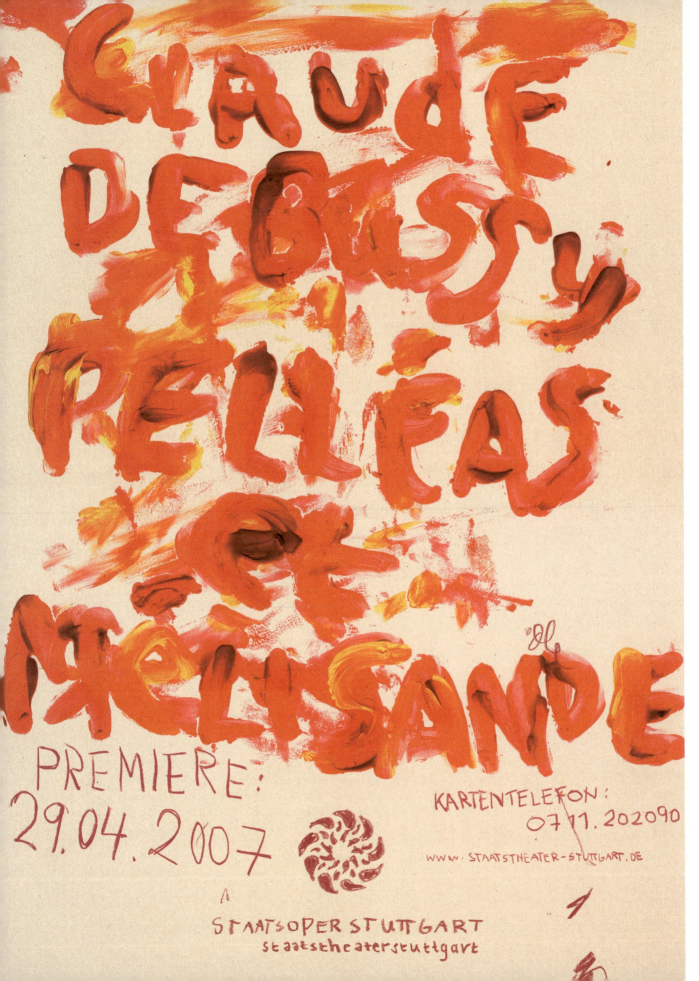

GEORGES BIZET

FRAGILE

CARMEN

800-295-5510

Parcels:
1/1

ORIGIN:
TEB

Sender's ref:
L35829, NYFST, 114685

F

TO: KRI
STR
SCHONL

DESTINATION:
STR

PREMIERE: 22.10.2007

KARTENTELEFON:
0711.202090

WWW.STAATSTHEATER-STUTTGART.DE

STAATSOPERSTUTTGART
staatstheaterstuttgart

7.0 /

GOOD DESIGN IS IR- RATIONAL.

.07

.07

Rational, more rational, irrational: nobody can explain good design to you. Your intellect is in the way. The only way good design can get to your head is through your heart. It is completely irrational – and therefore successful. If you follow the guidelines precisely, your design will turn out quite nicely but will never be exceptional. Heed the rules and break them with intuition and feeling: your design will set new standards.

Vernünftig, vernünftiger, unvernünftig: Gutes Design kann dir niemand erklären. Dein Verstand steht dir im Weg. Gutes Design trifft den Kopf nur durchs Herz. Es ist vollkommen unvernünftig – und deshalb erfolgreich. Wenn du die Regeln fehlerfrei anwendest, wird dein Design ordentlich, aber nie außerordentlich sein. Achte die Regeln, und brich sie mit Gespür und Gefühl: Dein Design wird Maßstäbe setzen.

7.1 /

Corporate Design
CLIENT _ STATE THEATRE STUTTGART

(2005 – 2010)

A POWERFUL
THEATRE

In 2005, the theatre logo featured heavily among the headlines of newspaper review sections throughout Germany. Why? Because it was fundamentally irrational. Artistic director Hasko Weber wanted to perform political theatre – and we thought that people should be able to see that, too. Over a bottle of wine we all decided that for the first season, which was set to start with Goethe's *Faust*, we would use the left-wing clenched fist salute for the state theatre in conservative Baden-Württemberg – at the risk of there being real trouble. And there was real trouble. We had agreed that if the worst came to the worst, we would explain that for the title *Faust* (German for '*fist*') we were unable to come up with anything better. Yet the calculated risk paid off: with a tailwind courtesy of the response to the new visual identity, the STUTTGARTER SCHAUSPIEL was voted theatre of the year during its first season.

Eine Faust für *Faust*: Das Schauspiel-Signet prägte 2005 deutschlandweit die Schlagzeilen der Feuilletons. Warum? Weil es von Grund auf unvernünftig war. Intendant Hasko Weber wollte politisches Theater machen – und wir fanden, dass man das auch sehen sollte. Bei einer Flasche Wein entschlossen wir uns gemeinsam, für die erste Spielzeit, die mit Goethes *Faust* starten sollte, eine zum linken Kampfgruß geballte Faust als Signet für das Staatstheater im konservativen Baden-Württemberg zu verwenden – auf die Gefahr hin, dass es richtig Ärger gibt. Und den gab es. Im schlimmsten Fall, so hatten wir es vereinbart, würden wir erklären, uns sei zu *Faust* eben nichts Besseres eingefallen. Doch das Kalkül ging auf: Mit dem Rückenwind durch die Resonanz auf den neuen Auftritt wurde das Stuttgarter Schauspiel gleich in der ersten Spielzeit zum Theater des Jahres.

Faust I
Johann Wolfgang Goethe

SCHAUSPIELSTUTTGART

Just as daring as the fist logo was the idea of selling programmes to theatre-goers for productions that they hadn't been to.
By cross-dissolving the cover pages and numbering the back pages, around 20 programmes per season were turned into a series – and became a collector's item.
Mindestens ebenso gewagt wie das Faust-Logo war die Idee, Theaterbesuchern Programmhefte für Stücke zu verkaufen, in denen sie gar nicht waren.
Durch Überblendung der Titelseiten und eine Nummerierung auf der Rückseite wurden die rund 20 Programmhefte pro Spielzeit zur Serie – und zu Sammlerstücken.

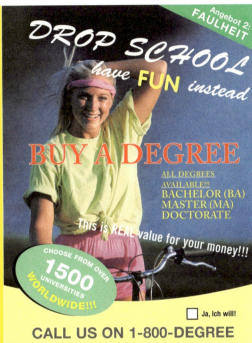
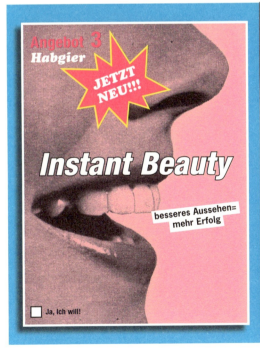
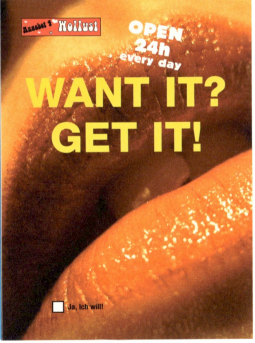

#1

Johann Wolfgang von Goethe _ *Faust*

SCHAUSPIELSTUTTGART
DOGVILLE

III

S: 14

SCHAUSPIELSTUTTGART
DOGVILLE

IV

S: 15

SCHAUSPIELSTUTTGART
DOGVILLE

V

S: 16°

#3
Lars von Trier _ *Dogville*

#62
Andrej Tarkowski _ *Stalker*

WORK

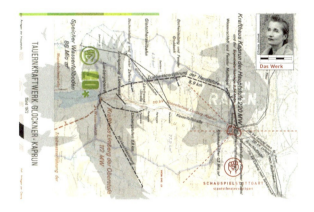

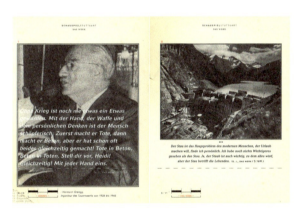

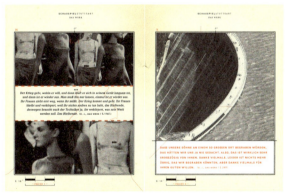

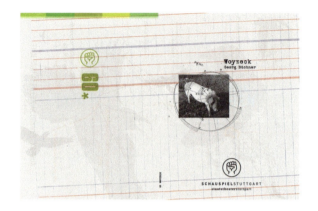

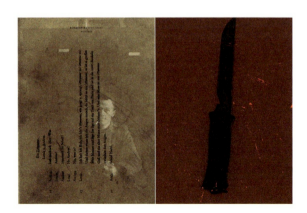

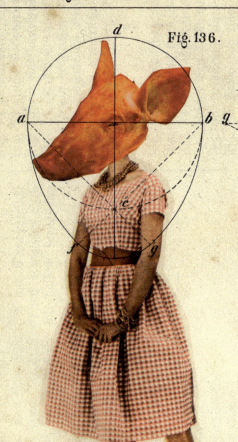

Abth.I. Fig. 136-148

Fig. 136.

Krätze, Flechten und andern Ausschlägen, auch bemerkt man bei der Untersuchung derselben keine Krampfadern, Drüsenschwellungen, Narben, oder venerische Merkmale, ausgenommen, daß der Kopf des rechten Nebenhoden sich etwas dicker und härter anfühlt, als gewöhnlich. Sein Auge ist nicht sonderlich belebt, aber von natürlichem Glanz und sein Blick fest, ernst, ruhig, und besonnen, keineswegs wild, frech, verstört, unstet oder zerstreut, aber auch

Abb. 42.1-4 Vier Augenpaare. Bei allen vieren zeigen die Augenbrauen einen kräftigen Verstand, wobei aber 1 und 2 den Vorzug haben. Keines dieser Augenpaare ist von einem aussergewöhnlichen Mensch. Hinsichtlich der Feinheit und der Empfindungskraft scheint 1 am gewöhnlichsten zu sein. 2 sind die weiblichsten und gütigsten Augen. Das Augenpaar 3 hat den zartesten und schwächsten Ausdruck. Das Augenpaar 4 ist am feurigsten, mutigsten und stolzesten.

#9
Georg Büchner _ *Woyceck* (2005/06)

WORK

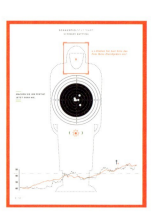

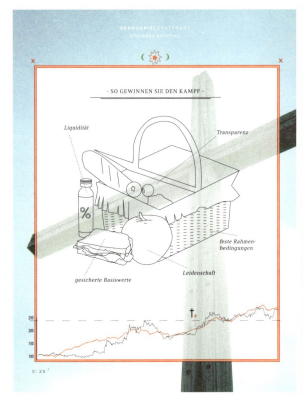

#10

Oliver Bukowski _ *Steinkes Rettung*

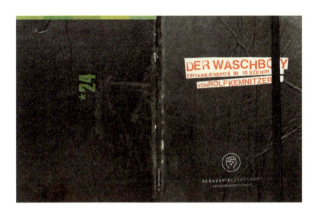

Rolf Kemnitzer _ *Der Waschboy*

#41

William Shakespeare _ *Wie es euch gefällt*

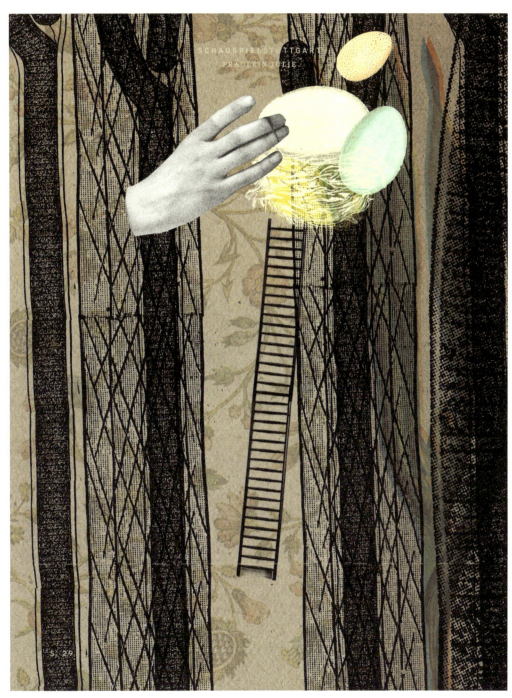

#45
August Strindberg _ *Fräulein Julie*

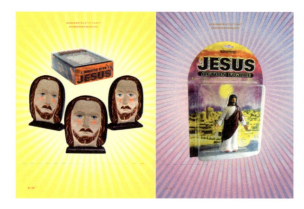

#49
Arthur Miller _ *Auferstehungsblues*

#32

Thomas Brasch _ *Vor den Vätern sterben die Söhne*
Rainer Werner Fassbinder & Michael Fendler _ *Warum läuft Herr R. Amok*

WORK

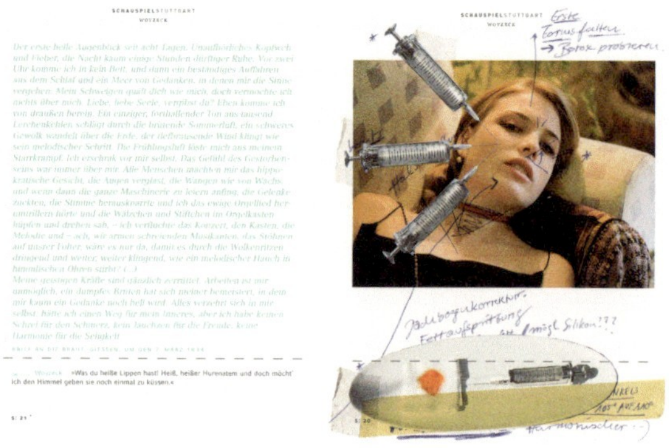
SCHAUSPIELSTUTTGART
WOYZECK
SCHAUSPIELSTUTTGART
WOYZECK
Botox probieren
Fettabsaugung

GEORG BÜCHNER
Woyzeck
SCHAUSPIELSTUTTGART
staatstheaterstuttgart

SCHAUSPIELSTUTTGART
WOYZECK

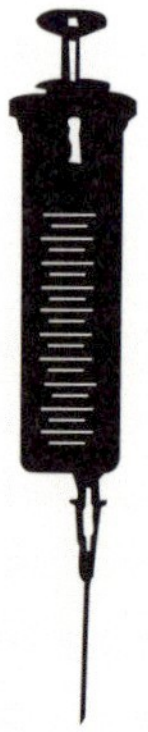

DIE NATUR HANDELT NICHT NACH ZWECKEN, *sie reibt sich nicht in einer unendlichen Reihe von Zwecken auf, von denen der eine den anderen bedingt; sondern sie ist in allen ihren Äußerungen sich unmittelbar selbst genug. Alles, was ist, ist um seiner selbst willen da.*

PROBEVORLESUNG ÜBER SCHÄDELNERVEN

✂ ..... Woyzeck: »Ich muß hinaus, 's ist so heiß da hie. Andres! Andres! wenn ich die Aug zumach, dreht sich's immer und ich hör die Geigen, immer zu, immer zu, und dann spricht's aus der Wand, hörst du nix?«

S: 11

HAUTPROBLEME
SCHAUSPIELSTUTTGART
WOYZECK
Höckerlangnase abhobeln
fliehendes Kinn
mit Silikonimplantat hervorheben
Isotonische Kochsalzlösung
0,9%
S: 13
SILIKON

#32
Georg Büchner _ *Woyceck* (2006/07)

SCHAUSPIELSTUTTGART

EINES LANGEN TAGES REISE IN DIE NACHT

meistgespielten Werke der Theaterliteratur und
wurde mehrfach verfilmt, u.a. von Sidney Lumet mit
Katherine Hepburn in der Rolle der Mary Tyrone (1962).
Christian Mahlow

S: 32°

#30

Eugene O'Neill _ *Eines langen Tages Reise in die Nacht*

WORK

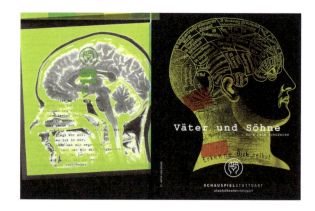

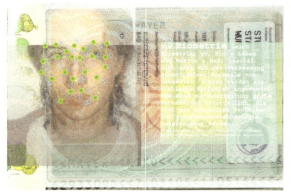

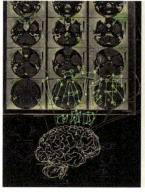

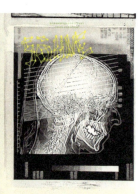

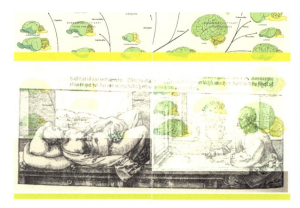

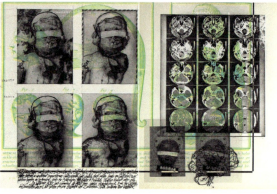

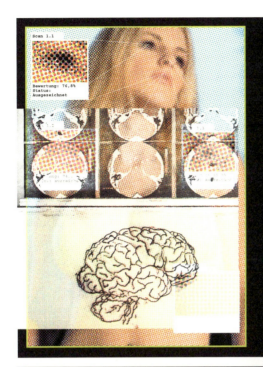

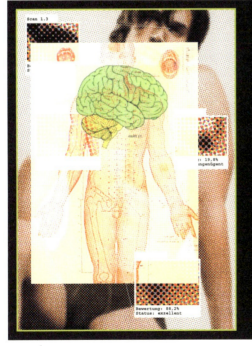

#19

Iwan Turgenjew _ *Väter und Söhne*

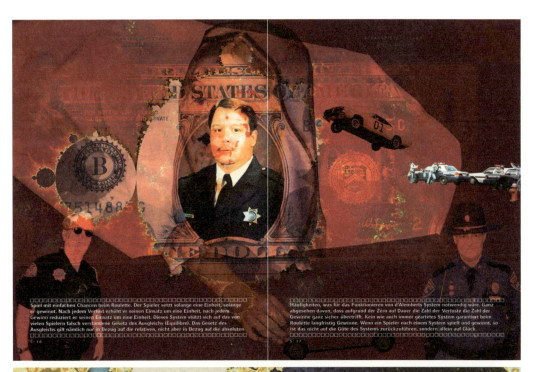

Spiel mit einfachen Chancen beim Roulette. Der Spieler setzt solange eine Einheit, solange er gewinnt. Nach jedem Verlust erhöht er seinen Einsatz um eine Einheit, nach jedem Gewinn reduziert er seinen Einsatz um eine Einheit. Dieses System stützt sich auf das von vielen Spielern falsch verstandene Gesetz des Ausgleichs (Equilibre). Das Gesetz des Ausgleichs gilt nämlich nur in Bezug auf die relativen, nicht aber in Bezug auf die absoluten

Häufigkeiten, was für das Funktionieren von d'Alemberts System notwendig wäre. Ganz abgesehen davon, dass aufgrund der Zéro auf Dauer die Zahl der Verluste die Zahl der Gewinne ganz sicher übertrifft. Kein wie auch immer geartetes System garantiert beim Roulette langfristig Gewinne. Wenn ein Spieler nach einem System spielt und gewinnt, so ist das nicht auf die Güte des Systems zurückzuführen, sondern allein auf Glück.

nimmt fälschlicherweise an, dass eine Chance, nachdem sie ein oder mehrere Male aufgetreten bzw. ausgeblieben ist, mit größerer Wahrscheinlichkeit auftritt, als die entgegengesetzte Chance. □□ **Algett:** Alvett war der Überlieferung zufolge ein orientalischer Mathematik-Professor. Die Alvettschen Figuren bestehen aus vier Coups der Einfachen Chancen. Aus vier Coups lassen sich bei mathematischer Permutation acht verschiedene Figuren und deren

Spiegelbilder formen. □□ **Ecart:** Wenn eine Abweichung von der Norm stattfindet, dann spricht man von einem Ecart. Dadurch wird die Chance zum Favoriten, die andere zum zwangsweise zu Restanten. Da eine normale Verteilung selten ist, darf bei einem Ecart nicht von einem Phänomen gesprochen werden. Es kommt natürlich auf die Stärke der Abweichung an. □□ **Fiktivspiel:** Henri Chateau erfand das Fiktivspiel, das nach allgemeinen

#35

Rafael Spregelburt _ *Die Dummheit*

8.0 /

GOOD DESIGN CAN CHANGE THE WORLD.

.08

Design is only seemingly about the visual – in actual fact it targets the subconscious.
We don't question what captures our heart. Good design is a potent tool: it changes our perception and consequently the world. It teaches us to love things and helps us to see things from a different perspective.
It is up to the designer to choose how they use their power:
the Red Cross is a powerful logo, but so is the swastika, unfortunately.

Im Design geht es nur scheinbar um Sichtbares – tatsächlich zielt es aufs Unterbewusste. Was uns ins Herz trifft, hinterfragen wir nicht. Gutes Design ist ein mächtiges Tool: Es verändert unsere Wahrnehmung und damit die Welt. Es lehrt uns, Dinge zu lieben, es lässt uns mit anderen Augen sehen. Es liegt am Designer, wie er seine Macht nutzt: Das Rote Kreuz ist ein starkes Logo, das Hakenkreuz leider auch.

8.1 /

Corporate Design / Relaunch
CLIENT _ STATE THEATRE STUTTGART

(2010)

POWER TO THE
PEOPLE

Due to renovation work, the SCHAUSPIEL STUTTGART moved for a year to premises immediately next to a highly controversial railway station construction site. One of the spokesmen for the protest against the state-run project was the director of the state theatre. Reason enough for us to give the theatre's corporate design a revolutionary makeover with a militant placard look in aggressive neon green under the motto *Metropolis*. The fist quickly experienced its second spring – and became a symbol of resistance against the planned low-level station. The giant fists from the construction hoarding around the theatre kept being cut out and turned into a protest banner; the neon fist on the roof of the theatre warningly greeted every train that passed on its way to the station. The Schauspiel may not have changed the world, but it did change the city. Even so.

Wegen Umbauarbeiten zog das Schauspiel Stuttgart für ein Jahr direkt neben das Gelände einer stark umstrittenen Bahnhofs-Großbaustelle. Einer der Wortführer des Protests gegen das staatliche Projekt: Der Hausregisseur des staatlichen Theaters. Grund genug für uns, das CD des Schauspiels unter dem Motto *Metropolis* mit aggressivem Neongrün und kämpferischer Szeneplakat-Optik revolutionär aufzufrischen. Flugs erlebte die Faust ihren zweiten Frühling – und wurde zum Symbol des Widerstandes gegen den geplanten Tiefbahnhof. Die riesigen Fäuste aus dem Bauzaun rund ums Theater wurden immer wieder ausgeschnitten und zum Protestbanner umfunktioniert, die Neonfaust auf dem Dach der Spielstätte begrüßte mahnend jeden Zug auf dem Weg in den Bahnhof. Das Schauspiel veränderte so zwar nicht die Welt, aber die Stadt. Immerhin.

RENE POLLESCH

von Rainer Werner
weitere Vorstellungen:
Premiere am 12. März 2011 im NORD,
01. – 03. April 2011.
Aufführungsrechte beim Verlag der Autoren, F...

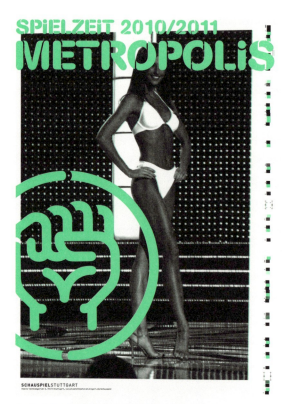

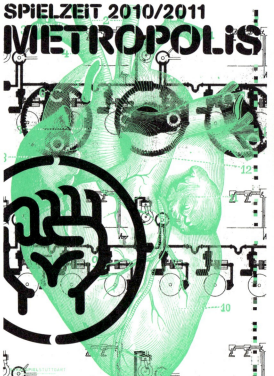

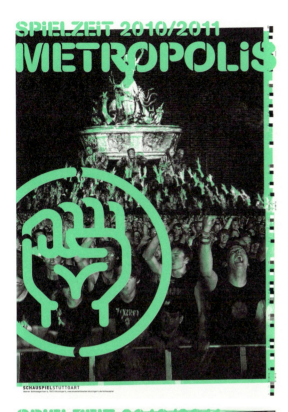

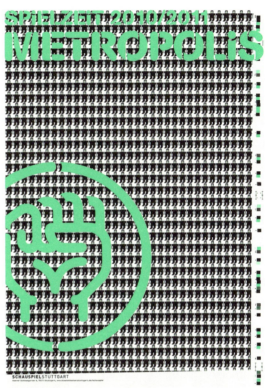

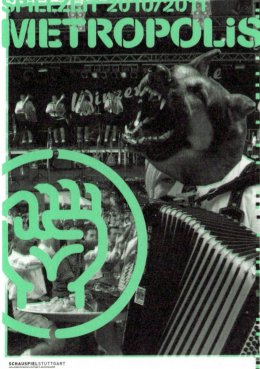

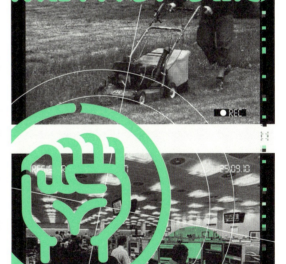

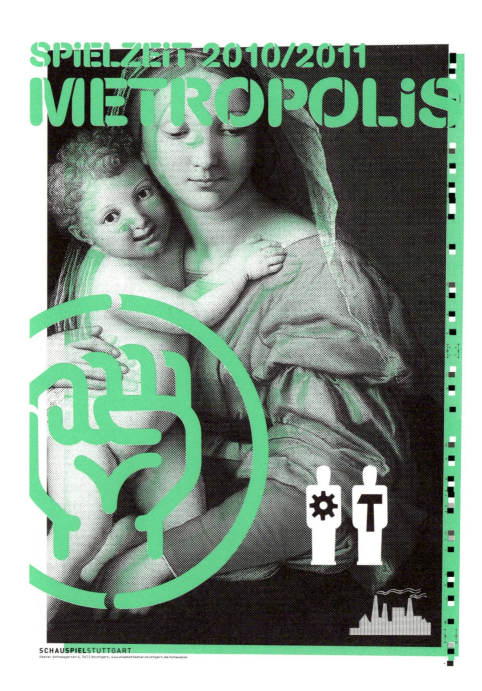

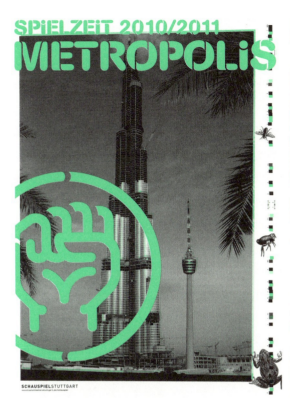

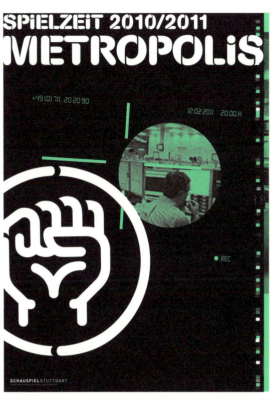

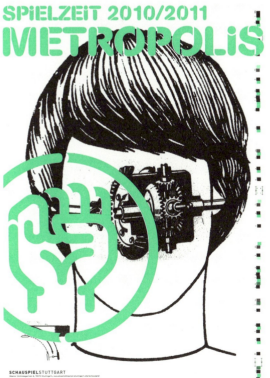

9.0 /

GOOD DESIGN IS MOSTLY ARTS, RARELY ART.

.09

Design in such a way that your creations can count as art – but never confuse design with art: you will fail. Art is creativity without a functional purpose, or a functional item whose outer appearance rises far above its functionality. Art is for the effect; design wants to be effective. Design that desperately masquerades as art is neither good design nor good art.

Gestalte so, dass dein Ergebnis als Kunst bestehen kann – aber verwechsle Gestaltung nie mit ihr: Du wirst scheitern. Kunst ist Gestaltung ohne Funktionsanspruch – oder aber Funktionierendes, dessen Gestalt weit über seine Funktionalität erhaben ist. Kunst will nur wirken, Design will bewirken. Design, das unbedingt Kunst sein will, ist weder gutes Design noch gute Kunst.

9.1 /

Corporate Design
CLIENT _ STATE THEATRE STUTTGART

(2009)

/ THE WORK OF _ STRICHPUNKT /

MAXIM GORKY
DOSS HOUSE

Over a period of five years we designed more than 100 programmes for the SCHAUSPIEL STUTTGART *(see chapter 7)* – all in pocket-sized A6 format. For *Nachtasyl* it took the form of an entire art book that illustrated interviews with citizens of Stuttgart with elaborate collages: a compendium of life in the city from the perspective of a taxi driver, a thief, a student, an entrepreneur, a short-time worker and other protagonists. Produced using artistic methods, but with a clear objective, too: thus some regard it as applied arts, some as art anyway.

Für das Stuttgarter Schauspiel haben wir in fünf Jahren über 100 Programmhefte gestaltet *(siehe Kap. 7)* – alle im hosentaschentauglichen DIN-A6-Format. Für das Nachtasyl wurde es ein ganzes Buch im Format eines Kunstbandes, das Interviews mit Stuttgarter Bürgern mit aufwändigen Collagen illustriert: Ein Kompendium des Geschehens in der Stadt aus der Sicht eines Taxifahrers, eines Diebes, einer Studentin, eines Unternehmers, eines Kurzarbeiters und anderer Protagonisten. Mit künstlerischen Mitteln umgesetzt, aber auch mit einem klaren Ziel: Manche sehen es deshalb als angewandte Gestaltung, für manche ist es trotzdem Kunst.

NACHTASYL STUTTGART

von Maxim Gorki und 33 Stuttgarter Bürgern

Textfassung von Jörg Bochow, Volker Lösch und dem Spielensemble

----

Premiere am 25. September 2009 im Schauspielhaus

Der Taxifahrer 16.06.09 28.06.09

~~Der Dieb~~ Der Zeitarbeiter 19.06.09 08.07.09

Der Dieb 20.06.09 09.07.09

Die Studentin 20. Juni 2009 06.07.09   Der Unternehmer 16.06.09 17.06.09 18.06.09 29.06.09

~~Der Sozialarbeiter~~

Der Sozialarbeiter 12.06.09 15.06.09   3.07.09 09.07.09

Die Ehefrau 17.06.09

Die Kranke 23. Juni 2009 24.06.09   Der Kurzarbeiter 18.06.09 19.06.09 26.06.09 05.07.09 07.07.09

Der Banker 20.06.09 23.06.09

Die Alleinerziehende 19.06.09 22.06.09 24. Juni 2009 26.06.09

SCHAUSPIELSTUTTGART
staatstheaterstuttgart

WWW.STAATSTHEATER-STUTTGART.DE

SCHAUSPIELSTUTTGART
NACHTASYL STUTTGART

DIE
ALLEINERZIEHENDE

10

11

S: 93

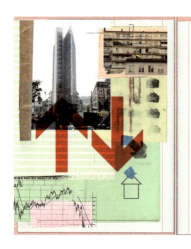

DER BANKER

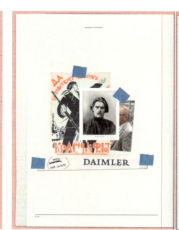

DER UNTERNEHMER

DAIMLER

DIE STUDENTIN

DER ZEITARBEITER

DER SOZIALARBEITER

DER TAXIFAHRER

9.2 /

Calendar
CLIENT _ BOSCH SECURITY SYSTEMS

(2010)

/ THE WORK OF _ STRICHPUNKT /

THE ART(S) OF
SECURITY

Valuable works of art around the world are protected with security systems from Bosch. That is why Bosch wanted to produce an art calendar. We focused on the Bosch systems themselves as works of artisanal art and illustrated them using artistic methods. Because quality and functionality have a lot to do with aesthetics – even if not everybody looks at that of a sprinkler system or a security camera in the same way.

Mit Sicherheitssystemen von Bosch werden weltweit wertvolle Kunstwerke geschützt. Deshalb wollte Bosch einen Kunstkalender herausgeben. Wir stellten die Bosch-Systeme selbst als Werke der Handwerks-Kunst in den Mittelpunkt und inszenierten sie mit künstlerischen Mitteln. Denn Qualität und Funktionalität haben viel mit Ästhetik zu tun – auch wenn man das einer Sprinkleranlage oder einer Überwachungskamera nicht immer gleich ansieht.

Fire detector

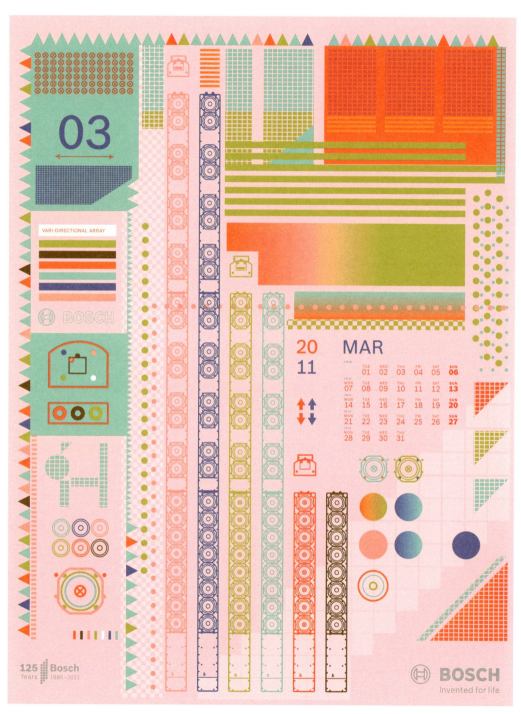

Vari-directional Array

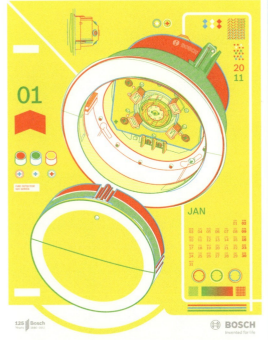

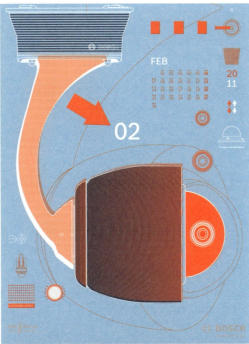

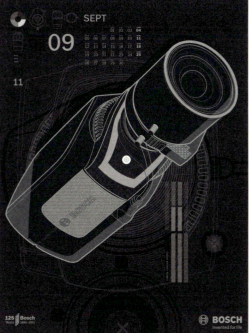

Fire detector, Autodome, Carephone, Dinion camera

10.0 /

GOOD DESIGN IS HONEST.

.10

Good product design is easy to identify: it works well and that is why it looks good. Graphic design is more complex: an incorrect text can be beautifully typeset; an untrustworthy company can have a flawless image. Hence good design does not embellish: it conveys character and values through the senses. A bad book that is beautifully presented betrays the reader. Good designers are honest people: they don't adorn things, they create.

Gutes Produktdesign ist einfach zu erkennen: Es funktioniert gut und sieht deshalb gut aus. Grafikdesign ist komplexer: Ein falscher Text kann herausragend gesetzt sein, eine unseriöse Firma kann tadellos auftreten. Gutes Design verschönert deshalb nicht: Es macht Typizität und Werte sinnlich erfassbar. Ein schlechtes Buch, schön gestaltet, ist Verrat am Leser. Gute Designer sind ehrliche Menschen: Sie dekorieren nicht, sie gestalten.

10.1 /

Annual Report
CLIENT _ CANCOM AG

(2000)

HANDLE WITH
CARE

In December 1999 we had a real problem: the management board of the Apple dealer Cancom asked us to design its annual report and to portray the company as a computer retailer that offered individual advice. As part of our remit, we obtained a thick study that stated precisely the opposite: Cancom was said to be no more than a low-budget *box mover* and that was the reason for its success. So we went back to the management board and presented it with a thoroughly honest *box mover report*: in a cardboard box, the foreword as a delivery note, the *facts and figures* section as a manual and the image section in an electrostatic protective cover. We printed the image section on cards that people could fit together however they liked – they could even construct something resembling an individual system house. Among the board members, there was initially complete silence, then everyone laughed their heads off – and the idea was subsequently fully implemented, using the company's own packing station.

Im Dezember 1999 hatten wir ein echtes Problem: Der Vorstand des Apple-Händlers Cancom bat uns, seinen Geschäftsbericht zu gestalten und die Firma als individuell beratendes Systemhaus darzustellen. Dazu bekamen wir eine dicke Studie, in der aber das genaue Gegenteil stand: Cancom sei vor allem ein günstiger *Kistenschieber* und genau deshalb erfolgreich. Also gingen wir zurück zum Vorstand und präsentierten einen grundehrlichen Kistenschieber-Bericht: in einer Pappschachtel, das Vorwort als Lieferschein, der Zahlenteil als Manual und der Imageteil in einer elektrostatischen Schutzhülle verpackt. Allerdings druckten wir den Imageteil auf Karten, die man beliebig zusammenstecken konnte – als individuelles Systemhaus eben. Im Vorstand herrschte erst Schweigen, dann wurde herzlich gelacht – und dann die Idee eins zu eins umgesetzt, passenderweise auf der eigenen Packstraße.

WORK

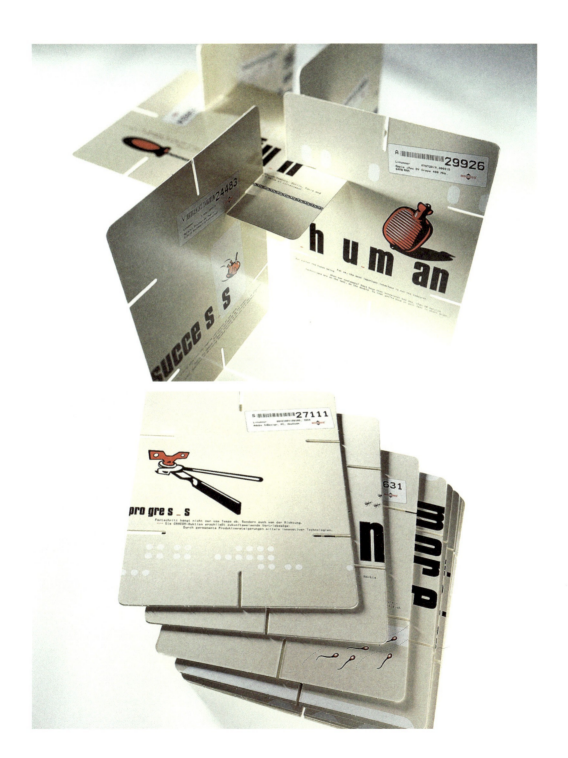

10.2 /

Corporate Design & Packaging
CLIENT _ EBERL MEDIEN

(2009 – 2011)

/ THE WORK OF _ STRICHPUNKT /

THE PRINT COMPANY
CHEESE

A leading printing company that supplies customers throughout Germany has a problem when it is located in the back of beyond – well, that's what they said, at least. We didn't agree: better to turn the problem into a solution and be proud of the fact that you come from the mountains. Together with the management we defined a new corporate structure, name and visual identity – and completely focused on the values of local ties. It's a nice thing that the family who owns the company has not only been producing media for decades, but also cheese, and that the authorised representative of the printers first tends to his cows on the pastures every morning. We celebrated this fact in a calendar. It is rather handy that the word ChEEsE has three Es – one for Eberl Medien, one for Eberl Print and one for Eberl Online. In 2011 we followed it up with HEimatsEitEn *(Home Pages)*, and 2012 saw a close-run race between BErgwEltEn *(Mountain Worlds)* and WandErwEgE *(Hiking Trails)*. The thank you we received from the company? Lots of locally produced chEEsE – what else!

Eine Spitzendruckerei, die Kunden in ganz Deutschland beliefert, hat ein Problem, wenn sie im hintersten Winkel des Landes liegt – sollte man meinen. Wir meinten dagegen: Man sollte das Problem zur Lösung machen und stolz auf die Herkunft aus den Bergen sein. Gemeinsam mit dem Management definierten wir eine neue Firmenstruktur, ein neues Naming und Erscheinungsbild. Und setzten voll auf den Wert der Heimatverbundenheit. Schön, dass die Unternehmerfamilie jahrzehntelang nicht nur Medien, sondern auch Käse herstellte und der Prokurist der Druckerei morgens erst einmal die Kühe auf seiner Alm versorgt: Das feierten wir in einem Kalender. Praktisch, dass das Wort ChEEsE außerdem drei E beinhaltet – eines für Eberl Medien, eins für Eberl Print und eins für Eberl Online. 2011 folgten die HEimatsEitEn, und 2012 lieferten sich BErgwEltEn und WandErwEgE ein heißes Kopf-an-Kopf-Rennen. Der Dank des Unternehmens an uns: natürlich jede Menge BErgkaEsE.

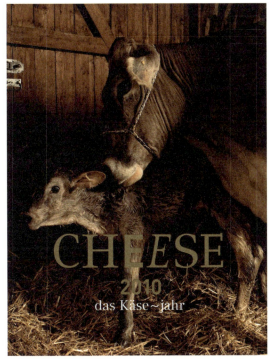

JANUAR
January

01
2010

		SKW 53	SKW 01						SKW 02						SKW 03						SKW 04						
01	02	03	04	05	06	07	08	09	10	11	12	13	14	15	16	17	18	19	20	21	22	23	24	25	26	27	28	29	30	31
FRE FRI	SAM SAT	SON SUN	MON MON	DIE TUE	MIT WED	DON THU	FRE FRI	SAM SAT	SON SUN	MON MON	DIE TUE	MIT WED	DON THU	FRE FRI	SAM SAT	SON SUN	MON MON	DIE TUE	MIT WED	DON THU	FRE FRI	SAM SAT	SON SUN	MON MON	DIE TUE	MIT WED	DON THU	FRE FRI	SAM SAT	SON SUN

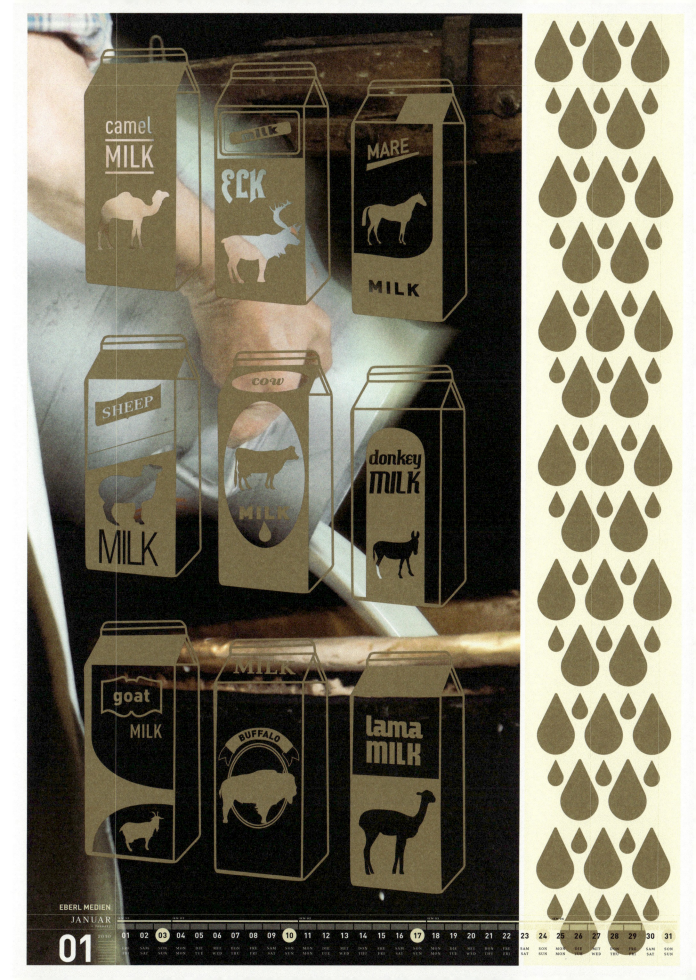

STEFANIES TILSITER

* * überreicht von * *
EBERL
SINCE 1859

50 %
FETT I. TR.

REIFEZEIT ~ 8 WOCHEN * * SCHNITTKÄSE

leicht säuerlich, würzig

JULI – July
07 2010

KW 27

01 DON THU
02 FRE FRI
03 SAM SAT
04 SON SUN
05 MON MON
06 DIE TUE
07 MIT WED
08 DON THU
09 FRE FRI
10 SAM SAT
11 SON SUN
12 MON MON
13 DIE TUE
14 MIT WED
15 DON THU
16 FRE FRI
17 SAM SAT
18 SON SUN
19 MON MON
20 DIE TUE
21 MIT WED
22 DON THU
23 FRE FRI
24 SAM SAT
25 SON SUN
26 MON MON
27 DIE TUE
28 MIT WED
29 DON THU
30 FRE FRI
31 SAM SAT

KW 28   KW 29   KW 30

MELKEN

QUARK

ZERKLEINERN

PASTEURISIERUNG

herkömmliche
Käseherstellung

Drainage
von Molke

VOLLMILCH (Rohmilch)

traditionelle
Käseherstellung

NORMIERUNG
UND FILTRATION

FRISCHKÄSE

SALZEN

RENNIN
(Enzyme)

ABGIESSEN
IN SPANKÖRBE

PRESSEN

AUSFLOCKUNG

BRUCH UND
QUARK

Drainage von
überschüssiger Molke

REIFUNG

SCHNEIDEN

RÜHREN UND KOCHEN

GEREIFTER
KÄSE

EBERL MEDIEN

JULI
July

07
2010

01 02 03 04 05 06 07 08 09 10 11 12 13 14 15 16 17 18 19 20 21 22 23 24 25 26 27 28 29 30 31
DON FRE SAM SON MON DIE MIT DON FRE SAM SON MON DIE MIT DON FRE SAM SON MON DIE MIT DON FRE SAM SON MON DIE MIT DON FRE SAM
THU FRI SAT SUN MON TUE WED THU FRI SAT SUN MON TUE WED THU FRI SAT SUN MON TUE WED THU FRI SAT SUN MON TUE WED THU FRI SAT

The calendar included twelve sheets for wrapping the local cheese specialities.
Der Kalender beinhaltete auch zwölf Käse-Einwickelpapiere für Allgäuer Spezialitäten aus dem Hause Eberl.

WORK

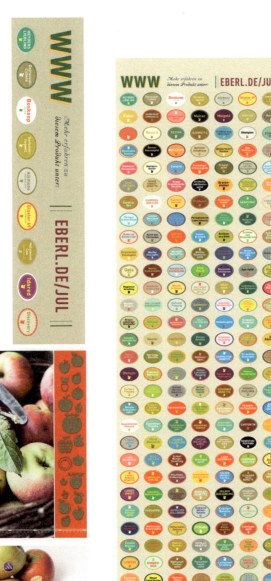

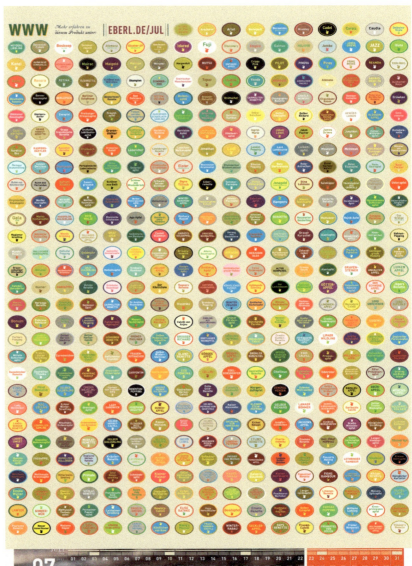

The following year, alongside the calendar, we also designed packaging for other regional specialities.
Im Folgejahr gestalteten wir parallel zum Kalender Verpackungen für andere regionale Spezialitäten.

11.0 /

GOOD DESIGN IS NOT FASH- IONABLE.

.11

Fashions are fleeting, style is timeless: good design cannot be trendy – that even applies to fashion design. Smart, newfangled goods may be nice to look at, but are never substantial. Good design never aims for short-term success – genuine innovations last longer than three months. Great designers create styles that outlive fashion trends. Black is the new black, and today's fashions are tomorrow's rubbish.

Mode ist kurzlebig, Stil ist zeitlos: Gutes Design kann nicht modisch sein – das gilt selbst im Modedesign. Schickimicki ist höchstens schön anzusehen, aber nie substantiell. Gutes Design sucht nie den kurzfristigen Erfolg – echte Innovationen halten länger als drei Monate. Große Designer schaffen Stile, die Moden überdauern. Schwarz ist das neue Schwarz, die Mode von heute der Müll von morgen.

11.1 /

Corporate Design
CLIENT _ NIMBUS GROUP

(2007 / 2008)

HERE COMES THE
LIGHT

What remains when you concentrate light and space on the essential? Clarity.
Based on this knowledge, we conceived an extremely low-key visual identity that provides a timeless stage for the
minimalist products. Beyond the corporate design we also clarified the structure of the group of companies and merged the brands
nimbus and rosso to form one visual identity – at the end of the day, partitions and lights are purchased by the same builders and
architects. However, it was less clear to us how many last-minute alterations there would be shortly before the opening of
important trade fairs – which led to us testing the lights under extreme stress on various night shifts.

Was bleibt, wenn man Licht und Raum auf das Wesentliche konzentriert? Klarheit.
Auf dieser Erkenntnis bauend, konzipierten wir ein extrem zurückhaltendes Erscheinungsbild, das den minimalistischen Produkten eine zeitlose
Bühne bietet. Über das Corporate Design hinaus klärten wir auch die Struktur der Unternehmensgruppe und führten die Marken nimbus und rosso im
Erscheinungsbild zusammen – schließlich werden Raumteiler wie Leuchten von den gleichen Bauherren und Architekten gekauft.
Weniger klar war uns allerdings, wie viele Last-Minute-Änderungen es bis kurz vor Eröffnung wichtiger Messen gab – was dazu führte, dass
wir die Leuchten in diversen Nachtschichten gleich selbst unter Extrembelastung testeten.

The Nimbus Group logo.

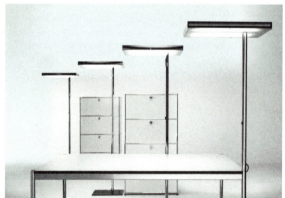

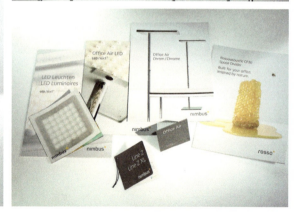

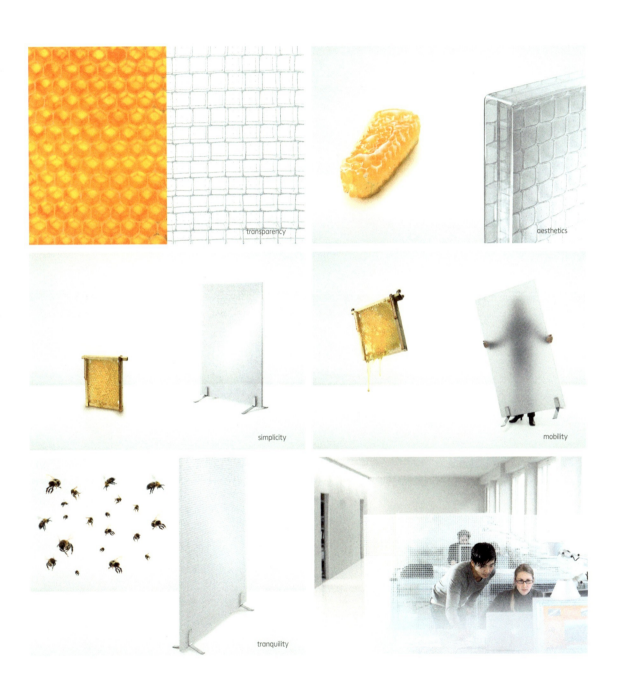

transparency

aesthetics

simplicity

mobility

tranquility

WORK

11.2 /

Annual Report
CLIENT _ AKTION MENSCH

(2011)

/ THE WORK OF _ STRICHPUNKT /

WE
CARE

An annual report is usually read for around three minutes. In our opinion, that was far too short for AKTION MENSCH, one of the largest organisations in Germany for people with disabilities. The solution was a tear-off calendar. 365 stories guide the reader through the year and ensure that the activities of AKTION MENSCH remain in people's conscience. This led to us designing the thickest report in the history of our agency, which absolutely paid off in a spiritual sense, although there was just one thing: when we carefully pointed out all the extra work it involved, it was charmingly countered with the remark that more money for the agency would mean less money for the pony stables at a home for the disabled.

Ein Geschäftsbericht wird normalerweise drei Minuten lang gelesen – das war uns für die *Aktion Mensch* – eine der größten deutschen Organisationen für Menschen mit Behinderungen – deutlich zu wenig. Die Lösung: Ein Abreißkalender. 365 Geschichten führen den Betrachter durch das Jahr und sorgen dafür, dass die Aktivitäten der Aktion Mensch langfristig immer wieder wahrgenommen werden. Dafür gestalteten wir den dicksten Report unserer Agenturgeschichte, was sich ideell absolut bezahlt machte, allerdings ausschließlich: Unser vorsichtiger Hinweis auf die Mehrarbeit wurde charmant mit dem Hinweis gekontert, dass mehr Geld für die Agentur weniger für den Ponyhof eines Behindertenheims bedeuten würde.

12.0 /

GOOD DESIGN CREATES APPRE- CIATION.

THESIS

.12

Good design is good business: if it looks better, it sells better. Focusing on mass instead of class destroys quality of life. Good design is not a question of price but a question of success – even on the mass market. When you eat, your eyes eat; when you shop, your eyes shop: design creates emotional added value. The difference between sobriety and sensory stimulation, between nodding and smiling lies in the quality of the design.

Good Design is Good Business: Was besser aussieht, verkauft sich auch besser.
Wer auf Masse statt Klasse setzt, vernichtet Lebensqualität. Gutes Design ist kein Kosten-,
sondern ein Erfolgsfaktor – auch im Massengeschäft. Das Auge isst mit, das Auge kauft mit:
Design schafft emotionalen Mehrwert. Der Unterschied zwischen Nüchternheit und
Berührung, zwischen Nicken und Lächeln liegt in der Gestaltungsqualität.

12.1 /

Packaging
CLIENT _ ADIDAS

(2010)

LIMITED EDITION
WORLD CUP SET

CREATING VALUES THROUGH DESIGN, PART I:

Imagine you are sitting in your office on a dull February afternoon picturing your dream job: it would have to be a totally amazing product with built-in fun factor, preferably for a global brand, with complete design freedom and no limits when it comes to production. Then the telephone rings: adidas enquires whether we feel like designing the packaging for the football shirts of six national teams for the WORLD CUP 2010. As a limited edition in the highest quality imaginable. The only catch: there are only three months in which to do it. It goes without saying that we stopped dreaming and got straight to work. For each team we designed a box that could be opened in a similar way to a glass cabinet. For adidas, the effort was worth it: the two-piece set cost almost three times as much as the shirts without a box – and was still sold out within a matter of days.

Mit Design Werte schaffen, zum Ersten:
Stell dir vor, du sitzt an einem trüben Februarnachmittag in deinem Büro und malst dir deinen Traumjob aus: Ein tolles Produkt mit Spaßfaktor müsste das sein, am besten für eine Weltmarke. Mit allen Freiheiten in der Gestaltung und ohne Limits in der Produktion. Dann klingelt das Telefon: adidas fragt an, ob wir Lust hätten, für die Fußballweltmeisterschaft 2010 die Trikots von sechs Nationalmannschaften zu verpacken: als Limited Edition, extrem hochwertig. Der einzige Haken: ganze drei Monate Zeit. Klar, dass wir zu träumen aufgehört und uns sofort an die Arbeit gemacht haben. Für jedes Team gestalteten wir eine Box, die sich wie eine Vitrine aufklappen lässt. Der Aufwand hat sich für adidas gelohnt: Das Zweierset kostete fast das Dreifache der Shirts ohne Box – und war trotzdem in wenigen Tagen ausverkauft.

Realising this globally managed project was no mean feat: layout discussions with adidas in Herzogenaurach and the football associations in Buenos Aires, Berlin, Paris, Mexico City and Madrid. Material selection, technical coordination and then production in New York, Eastern Europe and Asia. The individual design structures are a result of a combination of national symbols and the specific material structure of the adidas TECHFIT-shirts.

Die Realisation dieses global aufgestellten Jobs war nicht ohne: Diskussion des Layouts mit adidas in Herzogenaurach und den Fußballverbänden in Buenos Aires, Berlin, Paris, Mexico City und Madrid. Materialauswahl, technische Abstimmung und Produktion dann in New York, Osteuropa und Asien. Das Design ergab sich aus der Verbindung von nationalen Symbolen mit der spezifischen Stoffstruktur der adidas TECHFIT-Shirts.

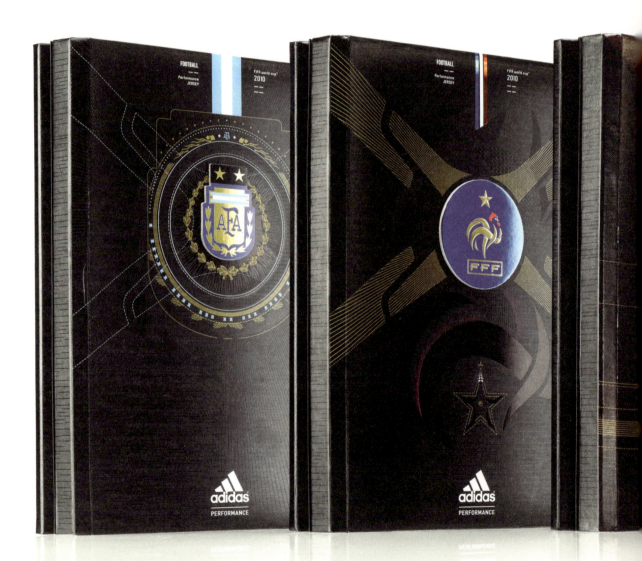

WORK

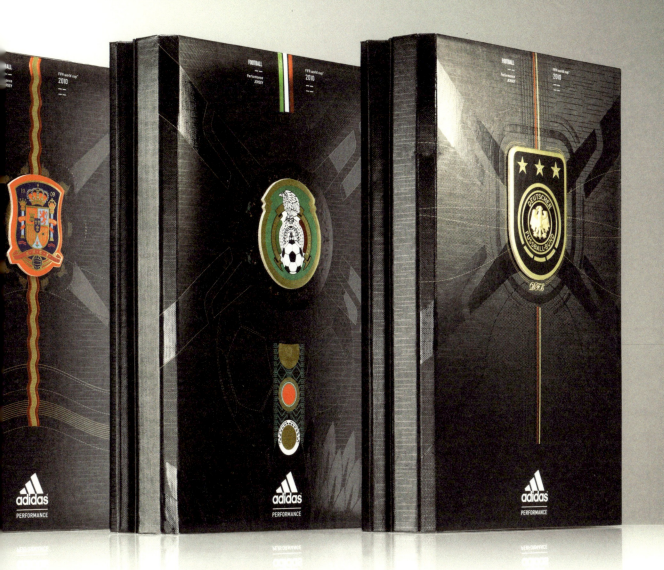

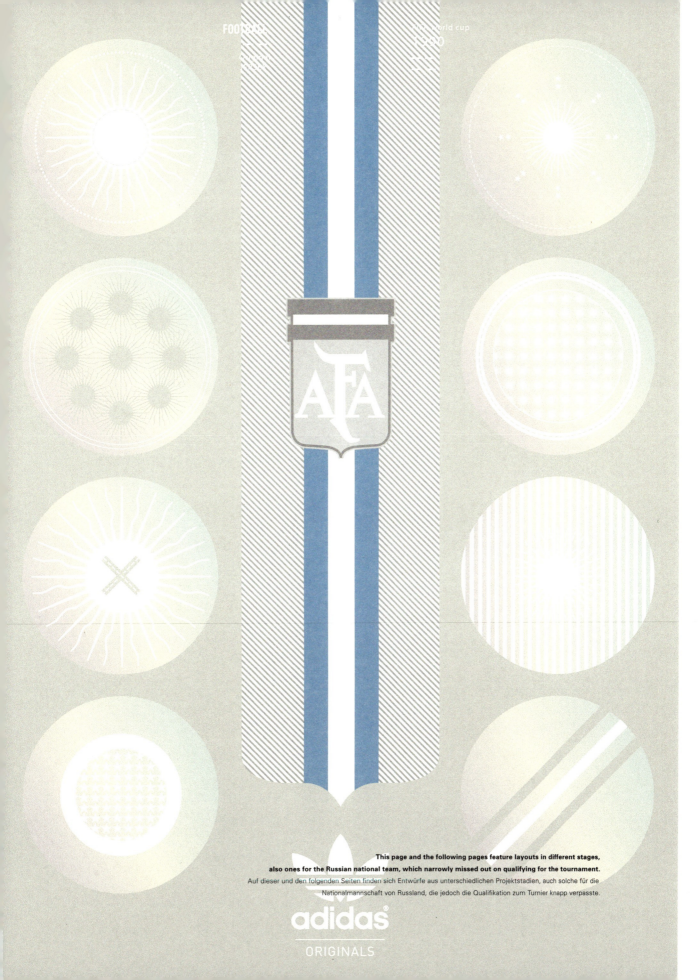

This page and the following pages feature layouts in different stages, also ones for the Russian national team, which narrowly missed out on qualifying for the tournament.
Auf dieser und den folgenden Seiten finden sich Entwürfe aus unterschiedlichen Projektstadien, auch solche für die Nationalmannschaft von Russland, die jedoch die Qualifikation zum Turnier knapp verpasste.

adidas®

ORIGINALS

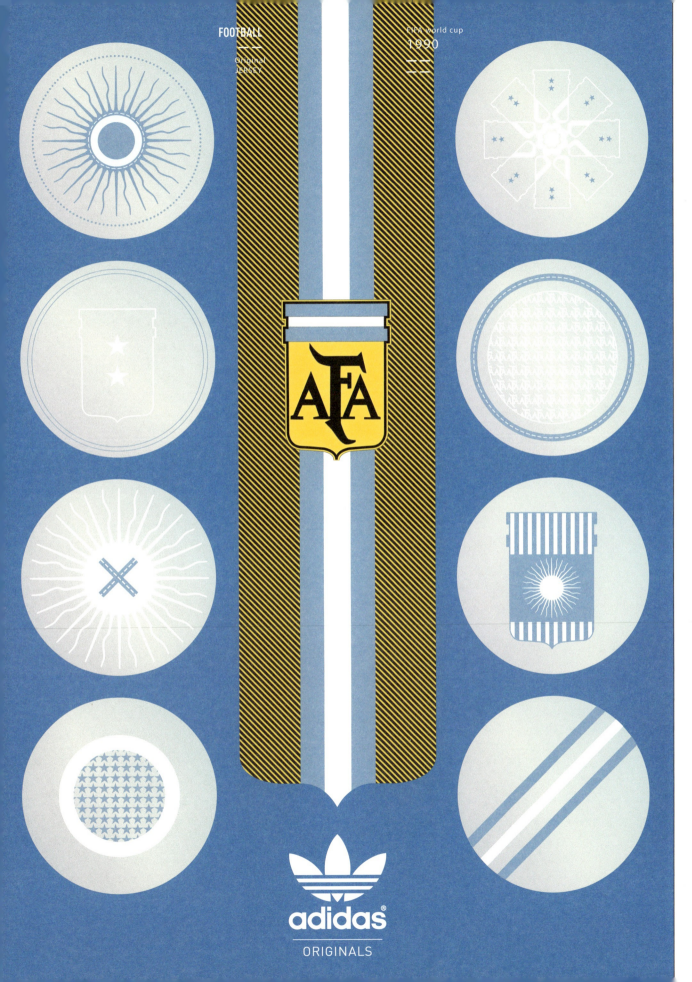

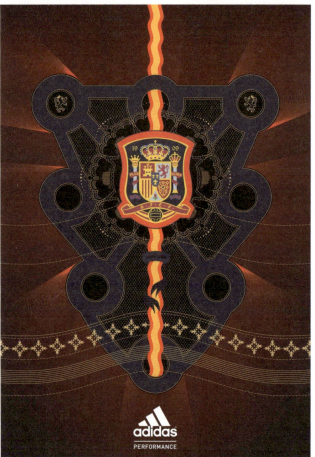

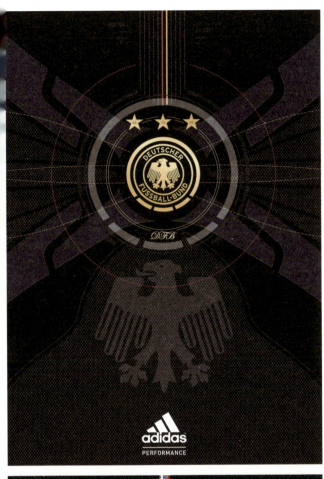

12.2 /

Packaging

CLIENT _ FÜRST LÖWENSTEIN / WINERY

(2010)

/ THE WORK OF _ STRICHPUNKT /

EDITION
C.A.R.L.

CREATING VALUES THROUGH DESIGN, PART II:

Less is more, when it is done right: the quality vintner Carl Friedrich, Hereditary Prince of Löwenstein, wanted to optimise the marketing of his best wines. His problem was the Bocksbeutel bottles typical of the region and the expectations of local wine lovers in relation to a traditional wine label. We got rid of the labels straight away, then printed just the first letter of the wine on the bottles. In doing so, we created a tribute to the revolutionary vintner prince: The 'C' stands for Coronilla, 'A' for Asphodill, 'R' for Reserve Hendelberg and 'L' for the Löwenstein Cuvée; together they spell out his first name.

Mit Design Werte schaffen, zum Zweiten:
Weniger ist mehr, wenn es richtig gemacht wird: Der Spitzenwinzer Erbprinz Carl F. zu Löwenstein wollte die Vermarktung seiner besten Weine optimieren. Sein Problem: die regionaltypische Bocksbeutelflasche und die Erwartungshaltung der Kunden an ein traditionelles Weinetikett. Wir ließen die Etiketten deshalb gleich ganz weg, druckten nur den Anfangsbuchstaben des Weines auf die Flaschen und setzten so nebenbei dem revolutionären Winzer-Prinzen ein Denkmal: Denn das C für Coronilla, A für Asphodill, R für Reserve Hendelberg und L für die Löwenstein Cuvée ergeben zusammen seinen Vornamen.

**Thanks to the transparent look, new sales channels have opened up in
cool bars and duty free shops – and a considerable price increase has been accepted by the market.**
Dank des neuen, transparenten Looks wurden neue Vertriebskanäle wie coole Bars und Duty-free-Shops erschlossen –
und eine deutliche Preiserhöhung wurde vom Markt akzeptiert.

12.3 /

Annual Report
CLIENT _ AIRBERLIN

(2008)

YOUR
AIRLINE

CREATING VALUES THROUGH DESIGN, PART III:

The image of a low-budget airline didn't suit airberlin, Germany's second-largest airline. So we changed all that – in the annual report. Yet changing values not only functions on a factual level, but, above all, emotionally (for more on this subject, see our book REPORTING). Accordingly, we interpreted the airline's various destinations with ironic image pairs and highly independent graphics and set the document apart from the grey mass of reports with diverse extras. The added value for the airline was the realisation that even analysts can analyse better when they are enjoying themselves at the same time. The added value for us came in the form of a merry evening with twenty thank-you Avernas at Borchardt's in Berlin. Per person, of course. Never before have we slept so well on a plane as we did on the way back.

Mit Design Werte schaffen, zum Dritten:
Deutschlands zweitgrößter Airline, AirBerlin, passte ihr Image als Billigflieger nicht. Das änderten wir – und zwar im Geschäftsbericht. Werte zu verändern, funktioniert aber nicht nur faktisch, sondern vor allem emotional (siehe dazu auch unser Buch REPORTING). Deshalb haben wir die vielfältigen Destinationen der Airline mit einer guten Portion Selbstironie interpretiert und den Bericht mit diversen Extras aufgewertet. Der Mehrwert für die Airline: die Erkenntnis, dass auch Analysten besser analysieren, wenn sie Spaß dabei haben. Der Mehrwert für uns: ein heiterer Abend mit zwanzig Dankeschön-Avernas im Berliner Borchardt's. Pro Person natürlich – nie haben wir im Flugzeug so angenehm geschlafen wie auf dem Weg zurück.

WORK

TXL → →   FOR FREQUENT FLYERS
YVR → →

RSW → →   FOR HOTHEADS
HEL → →

STR → →   FOR THE STYLE-CONSCIOUS
MLE → →

MUC → →   FOR CASH-COWS
JFK → →

WORK

12.4 /

Annual Report
CLIENT _ OCI

(2011)

DISCOVER THE
FUTURE

CREATING VALUES THROUGH DESIGN, PART IV

The world sometimes resembles a village – but with different districts.
That is why the Korean chemical company OCI consciously sought a European design agency for its annual report to not only
convincingly appeal to Korean analysts, but also the main players on the Western capital markets – and ultimately came to us.
As a result, we not only had the pleasure of talking about the best of both worlds whilst eating hamburgers and
wontons in Seoul with the boss of OCI. In relation to the design vocabulary, we took inspiration from the principal
materials that OCI produces: polysilicon and carbon. The design in landscape format with
shortened inlay pages combines Asian and Western reading customs.

Mit Design Werte schaffen, zum Vierten:
Die Welt ist manchmal ein Dorf – aber mit unterschiedlichen Vierteln:
Deshalb suchte das koreanische Chemieunternehmen OCI ganz bewusst nach einer europäischen Designagentur für seinen Geschäftsbericht,
um nicht nur koreanische Analysten, sondern auch die Akteure auf dem westlichen Kapitalmarkt überzeugend anzusprechen – und kam zu uns. Wir hatten
daraufhin nicht nur das Vergnügen, in Seoul mit dem OCI-Boss bei Hamburgern und Wan-Tans über das Beste aus beiden Welten zu sprechen.
Bei der Formensprache ließen wir uns dann durch die wesentlichen Materialien inspirieren, die OCI erzeugt: Polysilizium und Carbon.
Das Design im Querformat mit verkürzten Einlageseiten verbindet asiatische mit westlichen Lesegewohnheiten.

WORK

PAGE 14-15
2010 OCI ANNUAL REPORT

02
STRONG VALUES

Chance

WHAT WILL OCI MANUFACTURE IN 20 YEARS TIME? THAT IS EXACTLY WHAT OUR RESEARCHERS ARE WORKING ON.
THE FRUITS OF OUR R&D EFFORTS INCLUDE 11-NINE HIGH-PURITY POLYSILICON IN THE END,
WE SUCCESSFULLY RESPONDED TO A HUGE OPPORTUNITY.
WE SHARPLY INCREASED OUR CAPACITY TO PRODUCE A STRATEGIC PRODUCT.

11-NINE HIGH-PURITY POLYSILICON

99.99999999%

POLYSILICON PRODUCTION CAPACITY[METRIC TONS/YEAR]

17,000	27,000	42,000	62,000
2009	2010	2011	2012

PAGE 06-07
2010 OCI ANNUAL REPORT

01
FUTURE MARKETS

Future Markets 01

Photovoltaics.
Producing energy for a sun-splashed world.

SAHARA DESERT, AFRICA: DESERTS ARE A PRIMARY SOURCE OF SILICON, THE CORE ELEMENT OF OCI'S POLYSILICON BUSINESS.

PAGE 08-09
2010 OCI ANNUAL REPORT

01
FUTURE MARKETS

SIGLUFJORDUR, ICELAND: THE ALPINE GLACIERS HAVE RETREATED SIGNIFICANTLY IN RECENT YEARS DUE TO CHANGING ENVIRONMENTAL CONDITIONS.

What Color Is the Future?

PAGE 04-05
2010 OCI ANNUAL REPORT

01
FUTURE MARKETS

oci

The Future Is Bright White

It's bright white...

It's sustainable green.

It's powerful red...

And...successful black!

WHITE IS CLEAN AND BRIGHT—THE WAY WE ENVISION OUR COMPANY'S FUTURE.
BECAUSE WE DELIVER THE PRODUCTS OF TOMORROW.

WE PRODUCE POLYSILICON—A KEY TO CORE FUTURE TECHNOLOGIES.
WE PRODUCE FUMED SILICA VACUUM INSULATION PANELS (ENERVAC)—A KEY TO SUSTAINABLE, ENERGY-EFFICIENT BUILDINGS.
WE PRODUCE LED SAPPHIRE INGOTS—A KEY MATERIAL IN THE LED VALUE CHAIN.

FOR POWERFUL PHOTOVOLTAIC CELLS AND A WORLD FLOWING WITH CLEAN, SAFE ENERGY.
FOR ZERO-ENERGY HOUSES AND A SUSTAINABLE LIVING AND WORKING ENVIRONMENT.
FOR LOW-ENERGY, LOW-MAINTENANCE LIGHTING THAT MAKES OUR LIVES BRIGHTER, SAFER, AND MORE BEAUTIFUL.

WE DELIVER THE BEST QUALITY, IN ANY AMOUNT, FOR VAST, EVER-GROWING MARKETS.

SUCH CAPABILITIES HAVE MADE US A PARTNER TO THE LEADING TECHNOLOGICAL AND SOLAR ENERGY COMPANIES.
AND THEY WILL MAKE US THE LARGEST SUPPLIER OF POLYSILICON IN THE WORLD.

PAGE 16-17
2010 OCI ANNUAL REPORT

02
STRONG VALUES

"Our opportunity: sustainable ideas."

"OCI is constantly working on developing new ideas.
Our research teams are focused on three main areas:
Crystal growth, advanced materials, and green technology.
I am excited to be a part of this team, because
we are thinking about what and how OCI will manufacture
in 10 or 20 years' time. That is a huge responsibility
—but also a fantastic opportunity!"

SANG HYM WOO, RESEARCHER

"At OCI, the secret behind our world-class growth
is our world-class people. OCI seeks talented people
from around the world and provides a nourishing
environment for them to achieve their full potential.
Furthermore, our culture of excellence
helps global talents quickly acclimate
and perform their best."

FLORIAN SPROS
ASSISTANT MANAGER, VIP BUSINESS DIVISION

"Our opportunity: outstanding employees."

PAGE 18-19
2010 OCI ANNUAL REPORT

02
STRONG VALUES

Challenge

BALANCING GROWTH AND PROFITABILITY IS A CONSTANT CHALLENGE FOR EVERY COMPANY.
OCI HAS BEEN SUCCESSFUL AT MATCHING BOLD INVESTMENTS WITH SOUND FINANCES.
OUR RETURN ON EQUITY(ROE) PROVIDES POWERFUL PROOF OF OUR COMPANY'S SUCCESS.
AND OUR CAPITAL EXPENDITURES(CAPEX) WILL CREATE FUTURE BENEFITS FOR ALL OF OUR SHAREHOLDERS.

25% KRW 1,042 billion — 2008
28% KRW 849 billion — 2009
33% KRW 1,103 billion — 2010

CAPEX
ROE

"We set future benchmarks!"

OCI GUNSAN PLANT

13.0 /

GOOD DESIGN KILLS ADVER-TISING.

.13

Good design needs no advertising because it is inherent. Design fuses products and aesthetics; form and function; content and understanding. Advertising is part of the design – created for the superficiality of the moment: it adorns, promises, generates desire. Aesthetics is always decorative, function fulfils promises, understanding harbours the desire for knowledge. Advertising sells goods; design creates and sells values. Advertising is sexy; design is sex.

Gutes Design braucht keine Werbung, weil sie ihm innewohnt. Design verbindet Produkte mit Ästhetik, Form mit Funktion, Inhalt mit Verständnis. Werbung ist Teil des Designs, geschaffen für die Oberflächlichkeit des Augenblicks: Sie dekoriert, verspricht, schafft Verlangen. Ästhetik ist immer auch dekorativ, Funktion erfüllt Versprechen, Verständnis birgt Erkenntniswille. Werbung verkauft Waren, Design schafft und verkauft Werte. Werbung ist sexy, Design ist Sex.

13.1 /

Corporate Design
CLIENT _ SCHEUFELEN PAPERS

(2004 – 2011)

/ THE WORK OF _ STRICHPUNKT /

PREMIUM
WHITE

Up until 2003, the German paper manufacturer Papierfabrik Scheufelen had advertised itself to the printers who were supposed to buy its premium paper with a moderate degree of success. Then we were given the job of improving this advertising – and turned it down on the assumption that advertising doesn't get you very far. Instead, we showcased all the things that can be designed and produced on the world's finest paper. And these weren't aimed at printing firms, but creative professionals, who seek the best basis for the work they produce. A recipe for success for SCHEUFELEN and a stroke of luck for us – because who wouldn't want a customer who continually wants to explore the boundaries of what is possible? Who doesn't moan because the production is costing too much, but asks why we haven't added this or that refinement?

Bis 2003 hatte die Papierfabrik Scheufelen mit mäßigem Erfolg Werbung bei den Druckern gemacht, die ihre Premium-Papiere kaufen sollten. Dann erhielten wir den Auftrag, diese Werbung besser zu machen – und lehnten ab. Unsere Annahme: Werbung bringt nichts. Wir zeigten stattdessen, was man alles auf den besten Papieren der Welt gestalten und produzieren kann. Und zwar nicht Druckern, sondern Kreativen, die für ihre Arbeiten die beste Basis suchen. Ein Erfolgsrezept für Scheufelen und ein Glücksfall für uns – denn wer hätte nicht gerne einen Kunden, der die Grenzen des Machbaren immer wieder neu ausloten will? Der nicht meckert, weil die Produktion zu viel kostet, sondern fragt, warum wir diese oder jene Veredelung nicht auch noch eingebaut haben?

When we began working for Scheufelen, the company promoted 17 paper brands in 80 countries. Our first job was to have clear out! We reduced it to just five brands and standardised the overall look in order to strengthen the umbrella brand.
Als wir begannen, für Scheufelen zu arbeiten, bewarb das Unternehmen 17 Papiermarken in 80 Ländern. Unser erster Job: Aufräumen! Wir reduzierten die Marken auf fünf und vereinheitlichten den Auftritt, um die Dachmarke zu stärken.

In love – engaged – married:

A brochure for the *Consort Royal* paper brand (2008) featuring the basic principle of every Scheufelen tool: storytelling.
The reason for it: most designers and marketeers can't be inspired by showcasing only technical details, but by emotions.

Verliebt – verlobt – verheiratet:

Die Broschüre für das Papier *Consort Royal* (2008) steht exemplarisch für das Prinzip des Storytelling, das alle Scheufelen-Medien eint.
Der Grund dafür: Designer und Marketingentscheider lassen sich eher von Emotionen als von technischen Faktoren begeistern.

The *Values in Style* magazine for the phoenixmotion paper brand (2011) features stories about values in different branches like automotive, luxury goods, fashion, health care and food.

Das *Values in Style*-Magazin für die Papiermarke phoenixmotion (2011) birgt wertorientierte Geschichten aus unterschiedlichen Branchen wie Automotive, Luxusgüter, Mode, Gesundheit und Lebensmittel.

WORK

♀ MODEKONSUM VON FRAUEN **FASHION BOUGHT BY WOMEN**
~ **588 € PRO JAHR**
~ **588 € PER YEAR**

SCHUHE SH OES. OBERBE KLEIDUNG OU TERWEAR. DE SSOUS LINGER IE. HEMDEN BLO USE. HANDTASCH EN HANDBAG. SCHM UCK JEWELLERY. SPORTBE KLEIDUNG SPORTSWEAR. SO NNENBRILLEN SUNGLASSES.

♀ TOP 10 DER LIEBLINGSTASCHEN
TOP 10 BAGS

01 Tragetasche
02 Hobo Bag
03 Clutch
03 Turnister-Tasche
05 Frame Bag
06 Baguette-Tasche
07 Handbeutel
08 Duffle-Tasche
09 Feldtasche
10 Laptop-Hülle

01 Tote bag
02 Hobo bag
03 Clutch Bag
04 Satchel
05 Frame bag
06 Baguette bag
07 Wristlet
08 Duffel
09 Field bag
10 Laptop pouch

03

DIE BELIEBTESTEN LEDEROBERFLÄCHEN
FAVOURITE LEATHER FINISHES

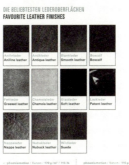

Anilinleder
Aniline leather

Antikleder
Antique leather

Blankleder
Smooth leather

Boxcalf
Boxcalf

Fettleder
Greased leather

Chamoisleder
Chamois leather

Glanzleder
Soft leather

Lackleder
Patent leather

Nappaleder
Nappa leather

Nubukleder
Nubuck leather

Wildleder
Suede

WORK

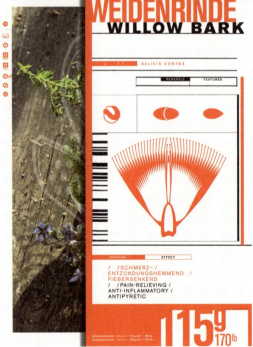

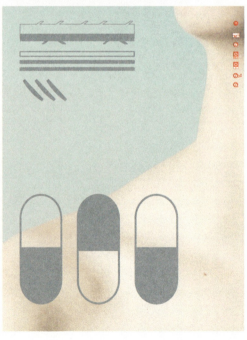

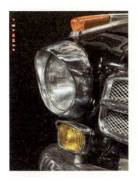

Please leave the light ON, BABY.

i ♥ cars

PHOE NIX MOT ION

Citroën B2

1920	Citroën

Sport Coupé

3683 mm	750	1653
1422 mm	kg	lbs

V4   1452 cm³

14 kW

21

PS HP

65 km/h
40 mph

sek sec   8 L

Ea -t SLOW

1 KANDIERTER PANCETTA & ZIEGENKÆSE 2
AUF SALATVARIATIONEN IN REIFEM BALSAMESSIG

RIB-EYE-STEAK AIX-EN-PROVENCE
MIT WEISSER ANCHOVISBUTTER, SAUTIERTEN ERDÄPFELN UND DELIKATEM GEMÜSE GEWÜRZT IN BALSAMESSIG

HALBFLÜSSIGER LONDON 3 SCHOKOLADEN PUDDING AN CREME DOUBLE

1 PANCETTA AND AGED BALSAMIC SALAD

CHOCOLATE PUDDING WITH DOUBLE CREAM

PREMIUM MENU \ PREMIUM MENU

LOU
CHA
OT

A UNIQUE ORIGIN

D) JEDES GROSSE KUNSTWERK HAT SEINE GANZ EIGENE GESCHICHTE – WIE DER EAMES LOUNGE CHAIR.

E) EVERY GREAT PIECE OF ART HAS A STORY LIKE THE EAMES LOUNGE CHAIR.

D) EINES TAGES befanden sich Charles und Ray am Set eines Wilder-Films. Inmitten der verrückten Ausstattung brachte Wilder, ein guter Freund von Ihnen, sie auf die Idee, ein eigenes Produkt herauszubringen. EINEN SESSEL, DER SOWOHL GEMÜTLICHKEIT ALS AUCH EINFACHHEIT AUSSTRAHLEN SOLLTE...

E) ONE DAY Charles and Ray were on the set of one of Wilder's films, a good friend of the. Wilder's slap dash rigs inspired them to think about an own product of their own. A CHAIR EMBRACING IDEALS OF COMFORT AND SIMPLICITY...

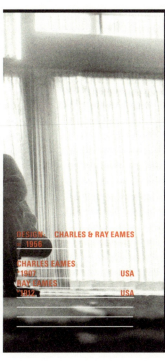

DESIGN   CHARLES & RAY EAMES
1956

CHARLES EAMES
1907   USA
RAY EAMES
1912   USA

13.2 /

Editorial Design
CLIENT _ SCHEUFELEN PAPERS

(2008)

/ THE WORK OF _ STRICHPUNKT /

HEAVEN
42

As dyed-in-the-wool Douglas Adams fans we had always wanted to honour the master: the introduction of a new, exceptionally white paper brand gave us the opportunity to do just that. We gave it the name *heaven 42* and sent a team into space to research unimagined answers to the question of absolute colour reproduction – and just as Douglas Adams solved the meaning of life, the universe and everything, the answer was '42'. In distant galaxies our astronauts also found total black. To demonstrate how this looked in print, an extra brochure was launched on the market under the title *back in black*, which made reference to our second secret hero: Bon Scott, the lead singer of AC/DC.

Als eingefleischte Douglas-Adams-Fans wollten wir dem Meister schon immer ein Denkmal setzen. Mit der Einführung einer neuen, besonders weißen Papiermarke war die Gelegenheit dazu gekommen. Wir fanden dafür den Namen *heaven 42* und schickten ein Team ins All, das nach ungeahnten Antworten auf die Frage nach absoluter Farbwiedergabe forschte – und so wie Douglas Adams die Frage nach dem Universum und dem ganzen Rest mit ,42' beantwortete. In fernen Galaxien fanden unsere Astronauten daneben auch das totale Schwarz, für dessen drucktechnische Ausführung eine Extrabroschüre unter dem Titel *Back in Black* auf den Markt kam – und damit auch unserem zweiten heimlichen Helden eine kleine Referenz erwies: Bon Scott, dem Leadsänger von AC/DC.

WORK

heaven 42 ®

> absolutely white

P. 10

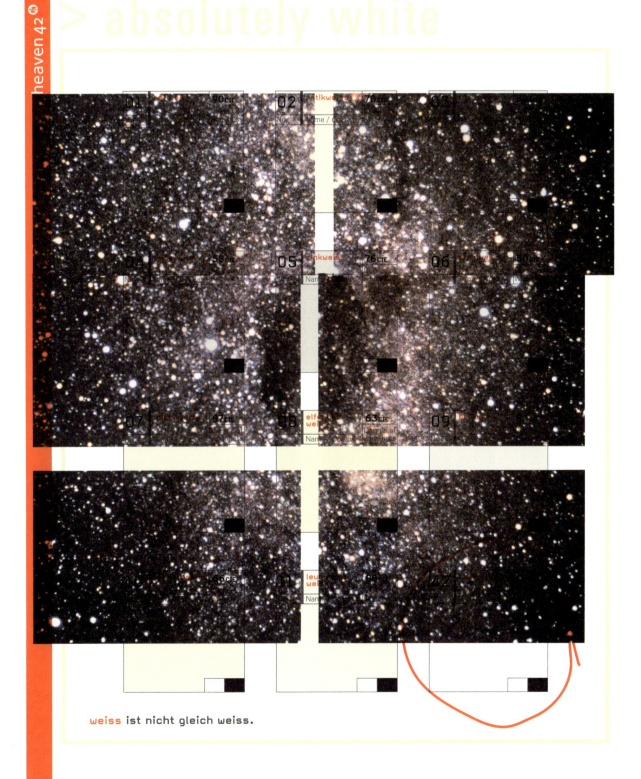

weiss ist nicht gleich weiss.

WORK

heaven 42 ⁴²

absolutweiss.

WE
IMPROVED
FOR
YOU:

farben
> wie nie zuvor.

155 CIE

125 CIE

WEISSGRAD
HEAVEN 42

WEISSGRAD
GESTRICHENE
STANDARD-
PAPIERE Ø

heaven 42 ⁴²

> the ultimate answer

P. 14

P. 5

www.heaven42.com/heaven42.tit

heaven 42 ⁴²

> softmatt gestrichen

SS / die neue dimension

RICHEN / FSC-ZERTIFIZIERT

softmatte oberfläche

ABSOLUT NEUTRALE FARBWIEDERGABE

meters (feet)		logMAR (VAR)

42 ABS

22 41 48

39 40 44 45

47 43 46 49

hoher kontrast = perfekte lesbarkeit

auch bei negativtext

und kleinen schriftgraden

38 (125)		0.8 (60)
30 (100)		0.7 (65)
24 (80)		0.6 (70)
15 (50)		0.4 (80)
12 (40)		0.3 (85)
9.5 (32)		0.2 (90)
7.5 (25)		0.1 (95)

heaven 42 ⓗ

P. 21

> absolutely white for the ultimate colour experience.

heaven 42 ⓗ

Der Orionnebel M42, erstmals fotografiert 2007.

WEISSE.

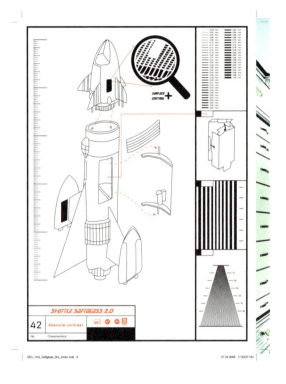

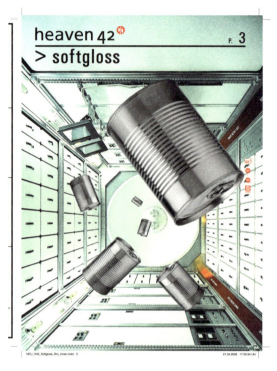

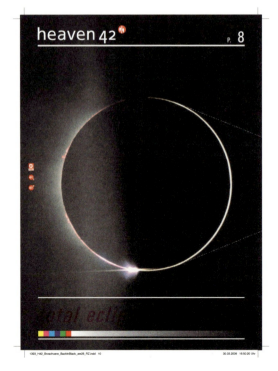

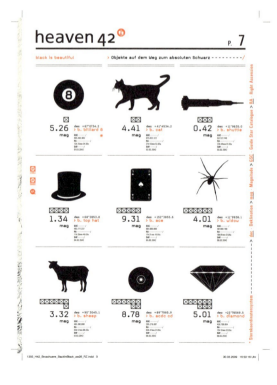

WORK

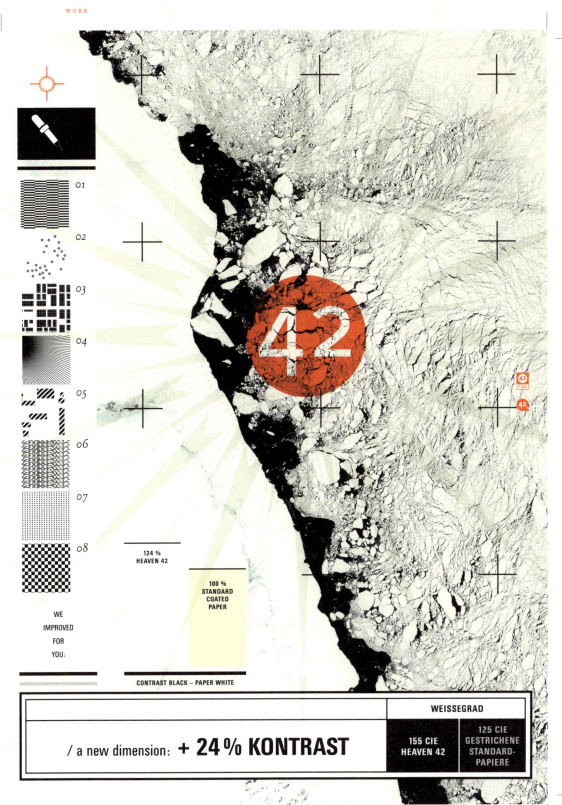

o1

o2

o3

o4

o5

o6

o7

o8

WE
IMPROVED
FOR
YOU:

124 %
HEAVEN 42

100 %
STANDARD
COATED
PAPER

CONTRAST BLACK – PAPER WHITE

	WEISSEGRAD	
/ a new dimension: **+ 24 % KONTRAST**	155 CIE HEAVEN 42	125 CIE GESTRICHENE STANDARD-PAPIERE

14.0 /

.14

GOOD DESIGN IS ABOUT SHIFTING LIMITS.

.14

Good design breaks new ground instead of tracing old paths. It develops perspectives where there were boundaries; it interprets anew instead of illustrating. Creation is the nucleus of design: creating something from scratch, something that has never been seen before. Design as the visual manifestation of common skills sheds poor light on the designer's capabilities, the consultant's assertiveness and the client's standards.

Gutes Design schafft neue Wege, statt alte zu beschreiben. Es entwickelt Perspektiven, wo bislang Grenzen sind, es interpretiert neu, statt abzubilden. Der Nukleus des Designs ist die Kreation: Die Schöpfung von Neuem, Ungesehenem, Unerhörtem. Design als visuelle Verwaltung des Gelernten, Bestehenden ist ein Armutszeugnis für die Schaffenskraft des Designers, für die Durchsetzungsfähigkeit des Beraters und für den Anspruch des Auftraggebers.

14.1 /

Calendar Design
CLIENT _ SCHEUFELEN PAPERS

(2005)

/ THE WORK OF _ STRICHPUNKT /

NONPLUS
ULTRA

To mark the 150th anniversary of PAPIERFABRIK SCHEUFELEN we set ourselves a noble goal: we wanted to show just what is possible in the printing industry these days. In the process we learnt that technical advancements aren't always the same thing as progress. For instance, current printing technology couldn't match the printing quality that was possible in 1855 shortly after the lithograph was invented – our benchmark was clear about that. The lithos from the collection of our friend Kurt Weidemann served as a basis for the calendar motifs. We supplemented these with contemporary design and wore out three reprographic service providers and two printing plants in the process. The calendar pushed the standards hitherto seen in the printing trade – and also inspired others: the anniversary issue of *Playboy* was published with the same cover sheet.

Zum 150-jährigen Jubiläum der Papierfabrik Scheufelen hatten wir uns ein hehres Ziel gesteckt: Wir wollten zeigen, was im Druck maximal möglich ist. Dabei lernten wir: Nicht immer heißt technischer Fortschritt auch Weiterentwicklung. Denn die Druckqualität, die 1855, kurz nach der Erfindung der Lithographie, möglich war, konnten aktuelle Drucktechniken nicht mehr erreichen – unsere Benchmark war damit klar. Als Basis für die Kalendermotive dienten uns Lithos aus der Sammlung unseres Freundes Kurt Weidemann. Wir ergänzten diese um zeitgemäßes Design und verschlissen bei der Umsetzung drei Reproanstalten und zwei Druckereien. Der Kalender verschob den Standard im Druckhandwerk – und hat auch andere inspiriert: Die Jubiläumsausgabe des *Playboys* erschien mit dem gleichen Deckblatt.

}

14.2 /

Calendar Design
CLIENT _ SCHEUFELEN PAPERS

(2008)

/ THE WORK OF _ STRICHPUNKT /

ONE OUT OF
24 108

For your eyes only

· · · · · · · · ·   EXPLANATIONS   · · · · · · · ·

SCHEUFELEN felt the full impact of the economic crisis in 2008 – which jeopardised the calendar that had been a tradition for decades. We subsequently decided, together with two printers and the publishing house, to produce this calendar on our own. The result was a calendar that, month for month, was as individual as its owner: the 2,009 copies contained 24,108 unique elements. From each of the 12 motifs on the elements fire, water, air and earth, as well as love, unique sheets were composed. We ran through over 1,500 variants on the computer until the design principle looked right. Then the sheets were produced in offset using 48 special colours and 12 finishing techniques and bound into calendars. A real experiment – with unique results.

2008 traf die Wirtschaftskrise Scheufelen mit voller Wucht – und gefährdete die jahrzehntelange Kalendertradition. Daraufhin entschieden wir uns, gemeinsam mit zwei Druckereien und dem Verlag dieses Buches den Kalender auf eigene Faust zu produzieren. So entstand ein Kalender, der Monat für Monat so individuell wie seine Besitzer wurde. Die 2.009 Exemplare enthalten 24.108 Unikate: Aus je zwölf Motiven zu den Elementen Feuer, Wasser, Luft und Erde sowie zur Liebe wurden einzigartige Blätter komponiert. Über 1.500 Varianten spielten wir am Computer durch, bis das Designprinzip stand. Dann wurden die Blätter in 48 Sonderfarben und zwölf Veredelungstechniken im Offsetdruck produziert und zu Kalendern gebunden. Ein echtes Experiment – mit einmaligem Ergebnis.

WORK

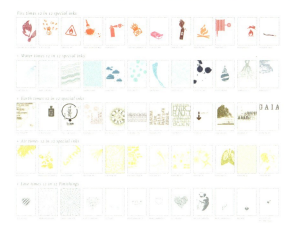

Fire times 12 in 12 special inks

+ Water times 12 in 12 special inks

+ Earth times 12 in 12 special inks

+ Air times 12 in 12 special inks

+ Love times 12 in 12 Finishings

5 ELEMENTS
60 MOTIFS
48 SPECIAL INKS
12 FINISHINGS
2,009 CALENDARS
24,108 ORIGINALS

HIGHEST VOLCANO: 6.880 m. Ojos del Salado (South America)

HIGHEST VOLCANO: 6.880 m. ojos del salado (South America)

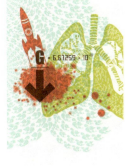

14.3 /

Poster Series
CLIENT _ SCHEUFELEN PAPERS

(2010)

/ THE WORK OF _ STRICHPUNKT /

PEAK
PERFORMANCE

The goal of every good designer is to constantly perform at the top of their game and make the best of every project. The client doesn't always see it that way. All the nicer when you are asked to design a series of posters on that very theme. We therefore rather immodestly brought together our *peer group* from all areas of society. The best thinkers. The most creative artists. The most successful athletes. And the most brilliant scientists. The tension grew with each new poster depicting these performers at the pinnacle of their profession, whilst also espousing the Scheufelen core values of creativity, premium quality and differentiation.

Jeder gute Designer hat das Ziel, permanent Spitzenleistungen zu erbringen, das Bestmögliche aus einem Projekt zu machen. Nicht immer sieht das auch der Kunde so. Umso schöner, wenn man gebeten wird, genau dazu eine Plakatserie zu gestalten. Wir haben deshalb ganz unbescheiden unsere *Peergroup* aus allen Bereichen der Gesellschaft in Szene gesetzt: die besten Denker. Die kreativsten Künstler. Die erfolgreichsten Sportler. Und die genialsten Wissenschaftler. Plakat für Plakat baut sich ein Spannungsbogen von Höchstleistungen auf – und unterstützt *nebenbei* die Scheufelen-Kernwerte Kreativität, Premiumanspruch und Differenzierung.

WORK

4 896 ¹L

3 042

KM
MI

_4.896 KILOMETER MIT EINEM LITER SPRIT
MIT EINER MUSTERGÜLTIGEN FAHRT BEIM ECO-MARATHON VON SHELL SICHERTE SICH EINE GRUPPE STUDENTEN,
DAS TEAM „POLYJOULE" AUS DEM FRANZÖSISCHEN NANTES, DEN ERSTEN PLATZ MIT DEM 1-LITER-AUTO, DEM SPAR-
SAMSTEN AUTO DER WELT. DIESER NEUE REKORD ENTSPRICHT DER STRECKE VON NEW YORK NACH LOS ANGELES ODER
VON DER PORTUGIESISCHEN ATLANTIKKÜSTE BIS NACH MOSKAU – UND DAS MIT NUR EINEM LITER SPRIT.

_4.896 KILOMETERS WITH A LITRE OF FUEL.
WITH A PERFECT DRIVE AT THE SHELL ECO-MARATHON, THE GROUP OF STUDENTS HAVING AT THE TEAM "POLYJOULE" FROM NANTES, FRANCE, MADE FIRST PLACE IN THEIR 1-LITRE CAR, THE MOST ECONOMICAL CAR IN THE WORLD. THIS NEW RECORD CORRESPONDS TO THE DISTANCE FROM NEW YORK TO LOS ANGELES OR THE PORTUGUESE ATLANTIC COAST TO MOSCOW – WITH A SINGLE LITRE OF FUEL.

 **Scheufelen**   (PAPERS FOR PEAK PERFORMANCE)

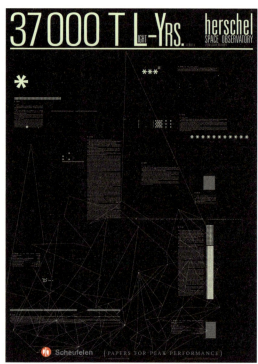

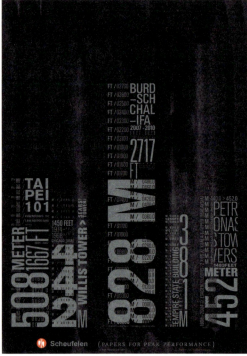

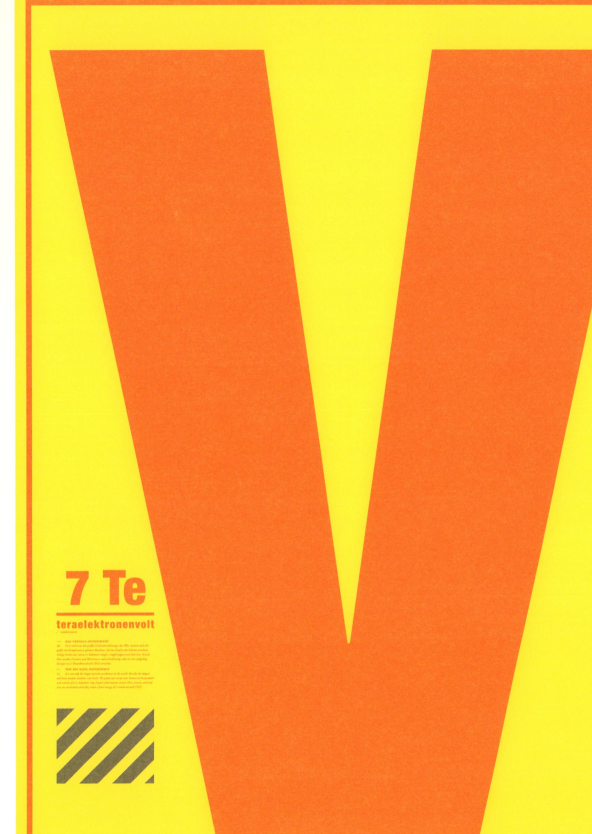

14.4 /

Calendar Design
CLIENT _ SCHEUFELEN PAPERS

(2011)

THE INNER CIRCLE OF
PERFECTION

One form, one subject: the circle. Uncompromising. Clearly defined. Infinitely practical. And it is everywhere you look: from the sun to sliced sausage, from the wheel to the eye's pupil, from the pea to the turntable. So what could be more obvious than dedicating the 2012 Papierfabrik Scheufelen calendar to this one subject alone? Particularly since the company's logo is thankfully also round – and therefore didn't have to be specially printed.

Eine Form, ein Thema: der Kreis. Kompromisslos. Klar definiert. Unendlich praktisch. Und überall zu finden: von der Sonne bis zur Wurstscheibe, vom Rad bis zur Pupille, von der Erbse bis zum Plattenteller. Was lag also näher, als den Kalender 2012 für die Papierfabrik Scheufelen nur diesem einen Thema zu widmen? Zumal das Signet der Papierfabrik dankenswerterweise auch kreisrund ist – und deshalb gar nicht mehr eigens eingedruckt werden musste.

03 /

2012

DIE SPEISEERBSE, THE
GARDEN PEA, PISUM
SATIVUM SSP. SATIVUM, /sub-
UNTERARTEN /species

PALERBSE/
ROUND PEA/
VAR. SATIVUM/

MARKERBSE/
WRINKLED PEA/
VAR. MEDULLARE/

ZUCKERERBSE/
SUGAR PEA/
VAR. SACCHARATUM/

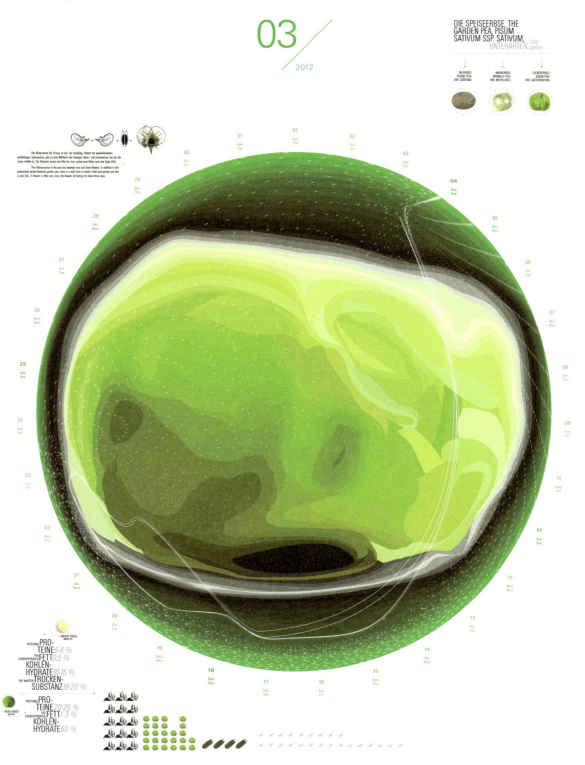

Der Blütenstand der Erbsen ist ein- bis dreiblütig. Neben der weissbraunen-
weißblütigen Speiseerbse, gibt es eine Wildform der heutigen Acker- und Gartenerbse, bei der die
Fahne hellila ist. Die Blütezeit dauert von Mai bis Juni, wobei eine Blüte rund drei Tage blüht.

The inflorescence of the pea has between one and three flowers. In addition to the
widespread white-flowered garden pea, there is a wild form of today's field and garden pea that
is pale lilac, it flowers in May and June, the flowers all lasting for about three days.

PROTEINE/PRO-
TEINE 5-8 %
FETT/FETT 0,5 %
CARBOHYDRATES/
KOHLEN-
HYDRATE 10-15 %
DRY MATTER/TROCKEN-
SUBSTANZ 18-20 %

PROTEINS/PRO-
TEINE 20-25 %
FAT/FETT 1-3 %
CARBOHYDRATES/
KOHLEN-
HYDRATE 60 %

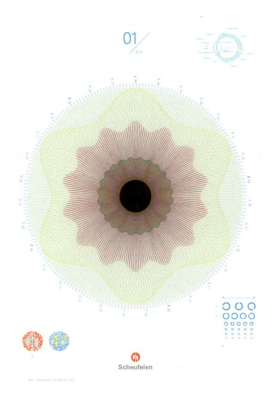

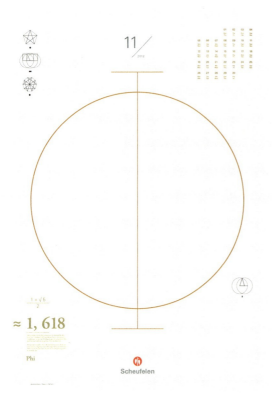

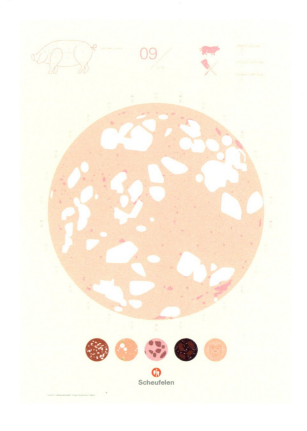

WORK

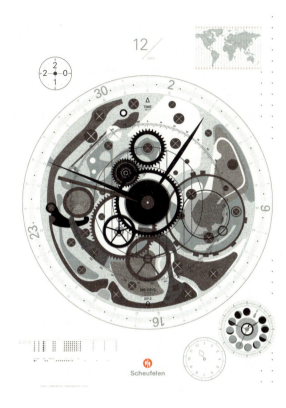

10/

2012

⌀

3476 KM

MONDPHASEN

phases of the moon

NEUMOND 1 **ZUNEHMENDER MOND** 2-4
VOLLMOND 5 **ABNEHMENDER MOND** 6-8
HALBMOND ZUNEHMEND 3 **ABNEHMEND** 7

01	02	03	04	05	06	**07**	08	09	10	11	12	13	**14**	15	16	17	18	19	20	**21**	22	23
Mon	Die	Mit	Don	Fre	Sam	**Son**	Mon	Die	Mit	Don	Fre	Sam	**Son**	Mon	Die	Mit	Don	Fre	Sam	**Son**	Mon	Die
Mon	Tue	Wed	Thu	Fri	Sat	**Sun**	Mon	Tue	Wed	Thu	Fri	Sat	**Sun**	Mon	Tue	Wed	Thu	Fri	Sat	**Sun**	Mon	Tue

24	25	26	27	**28**	29	30	31
Mit	Don	Fre	Sam	**Son**	Mon	Die	Mit
Wed	Thu	Fri	Sat	**Sun**	Mon	Tue	Wed

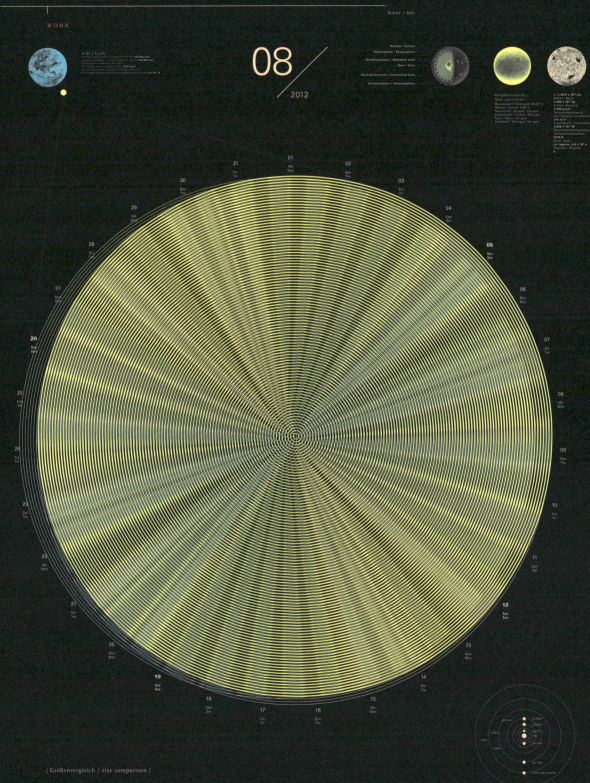

Sonne / Sun

WORK

08 /

2012

[Größenvergleich / size comparison]

Jupiter   Saturn   Uranus   Neptun   Erde   Venus   Mars   Merkur   Pluto

15.0 /

GOOD DESIGN IS RADICAL.

.15

Good design has absolute quality standards. Imbued with the lifeblood of its creator, it is the visible expression of their creative power and will, the product of a relentless struggle with the subject matter and the self. Good design is always a deed, never an attempt. It is always a solution, never a compromise. Good design is radical. Right. And extremely rare, but it is always worth the journey.

Gutes Design hat absoluten Qualitätsanspruch. Vom Herzblut des Gestalters durchtränkt, ist es sichtbarer Ausdruck seiner Kreations- und Willenskraft, Produkt eines unerbittlichen Kampfes mit der Materie und sich selbst. Gutes Design ist immer Tat, nie Versuch. Ist immer Lösung, nie Kompromiss. Gutes Design ist radikal. Richtig. Und extrem selten, aber den Weg immer wert.

15.1 /

Diary
CLIENT _ SCHEUFELEN PAPERS

(2003)

HEARTBEAT
MOMENTS

Our idea: we wanted to show what the paper *phoenixmotion* is most suitable for – conveying everything that is close to the hearts of designers and their clients. So that these things would also remain there for a whole year, we created the *Heartbeat Diary:* a desk calendar with 12 stories about the heart. The US head of marketing at the paper company announced, however, that he would personally tear out the pages featuring the photos of the carefully considered animal hearts: in his view, in the land of reformed meat this was an absolute no-go. Yet he overlooked a couple of pages – and so, of all the pages that could have been projected onto a big screen at a gala dinner as part of the Design Grand Prix at the New York Festival, it had to be the animal hearts.

Unsere Idee: Wir wollten zeigen, wozu das Papier *phoenixmotion* am besten geeignet ist – nämlich all das zu transportieren, was Gestaltern und deren Kunden wirklich am Herzen liegt. Damit es dort auch ein ganzes Jahr bleibt, kreierten wir das *Heartbeat Diary:* einen Tischkalender mit zwölf Geschichten rund ums Herz. Der US-Marketingleiter der Papierfabrik kündigte allerdings an, die Seiten mit Fotos fein säuberlich abgewogener Tierherzen persönlich herauszureißen: Im Land des Formfleisches war das aus seiner Sicht ein absolutes No-go. Ein paar Seiten hatte er dann doch übersehen – und so wurden beim Galadiner zum Design-Grand-Prix der New York Festivals ausgerechnet die Tierherzen großflächig projiziert.

WORK

Some design purists regard it as an insult to the logo, we regard it as a proof of its power: in every Scheufelen brochure, we use variations of the respective product logo on every page to explain the different printing and finishing techniques.
Manche Designpuristen empfinden es als Verbrechen am Signet, wir sehen es als Beweis seiner Stärke: In allen Scheufelen-Medien nutzen wir Variationen des jeweiligen Markenzeichens, um auf jeder Seite die genutzten Druck- und Veredelungstechniken zu erläutern.

Xantic 170 g/m^2 // 115lb text

-- >>> / 5 unterschiedliche / 5 different / 5 différents / 5 diverse

GRAMMATUREN / BASIS WEIGHTS / GRAMMAGES / GRAMMATURE ←

(115 g/m^2 -- 78lb text // 135 g/m^2 -- 90lb text // 150 g/m^2 -- 100lb text // 170 g/m^2 -- 115lb text // 250 g/m^2 -- 93lb cover)

ALWAYS ON THE RIGHT SIDE OF WEIGHT

------ **X**enon
------ **X**antur
------ **X**antic

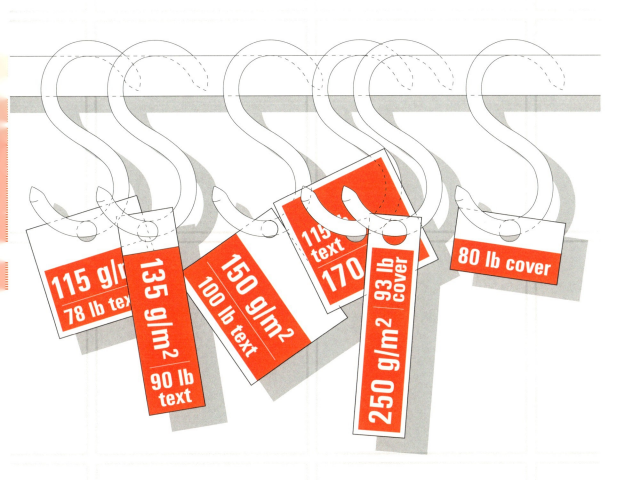

115 g/m ... 78 lb text

135 g/m^2 90 lb text

150 g/m^2 100 lb text

115 text 170

250 g/m^2 93 lb cover

80 lb cover

WORK

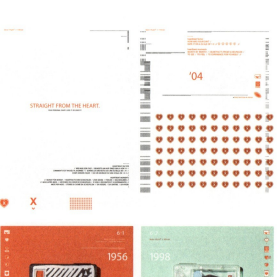

STRAIGHT FROM THE HEART.

'04

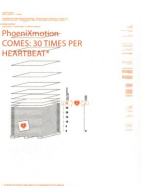

PhoeniXmotion
COMES: 30 TIMES PER
HEARTBEAT*

1956

1998

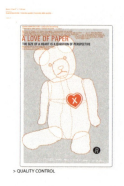

A LOVE OF PAPER
THE SIZE OF A HEART IS A QUESTION OF PERSPECTIVE

> QUALITY CONTROL

07-08

MOMENT # 08

80% OF SAILORS HAVE A TATTOO.
84% OF THEM HAVE A HEART TATTOO.

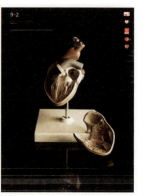

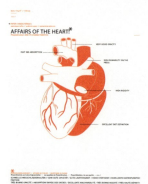

AFFAIRS OF THE HEART!*

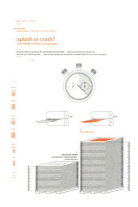

15.2 /

Diary
CLIENT _ SCHEUFELEN PAPERS

(2004)

THE
SUMMIT BOOK

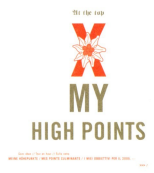

The *Heartbeat Diary* quickly found a place in the hearts of the clients – so diary number two followed the year after. We raised the bar higher, of course – because as everyone knows, the higher you go, the faster your heart beats. The *Summit Book* provides instructions on how to reach peaks and pinnacles. Setbacks are also considered, for instance time delays caused by bumping into Heidi, which can lead to peaks of quite a different kind.

Das *Heartbeat Diary* hatte schnell einen festen Platz in den Herzen der Kunden gefunden – also folgte im Jahr darauf Diary Nummer zwei, natürlich mit einer Steigerung – und die führt bekanntlich stets aufwärts, denn ganz oben schlagen die Herzen höher. Das *Gipfelbuch* bietet Anleitungen zur Erreichung von Höhepunkten. Rückschläge werden dabei auch berücksichtigt, zum Beispiel Zeitverzögerungen bei der Begegnung mit Heidi, die zu Höhepunkten ganz anderer Art führen können.

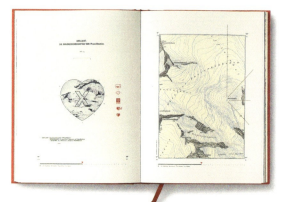

WORK

(don't panic):

DON'T GIVE UP!

PhoeniXmotion:
RESCUES THE PRINTED IMAGE
(INK CONSUMPTION COMPARED WITH UNCOATED PAPERS)

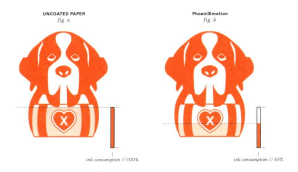

UNCOATED PAPER
fig. a

PhoeniXmotion
fig. b

ink consumption // 100%   *ink consumption // 65%*

'65"
—
0 m

'65"
—
▲

01 -- *die Rückschläge / the setbacks / les revers / le sconfitte*

X
THE
MOUNTAIN
IS CALLING!

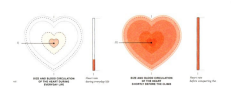

**Even here *(see chapter 13.2)* a small, personal highlight in the otherwise dreary existence of a designer during lonely
night shifts survived the rigorous editing process: the headlines for the seductive mountain pasture rendezvous are all titles of AC/DC songs.**

Auch hier *(siehe Kap. 13.2)* hat ein kleiner persönlicher Höhepunkt des trostlosen Designerdaseins während einsamer Nachtschichten das harte
Lektorat überlebt: Die Headlines zum verführerischen Alm-Rendezvous sind ausnahmslos Titel von AC/DC-Songs.

WORK

PhoeniXmotion:
HIGH RIGIDITY.

PhoeniXmotion
'05

NATURAL:
THE SURFACE OF PhoeniXmotion.

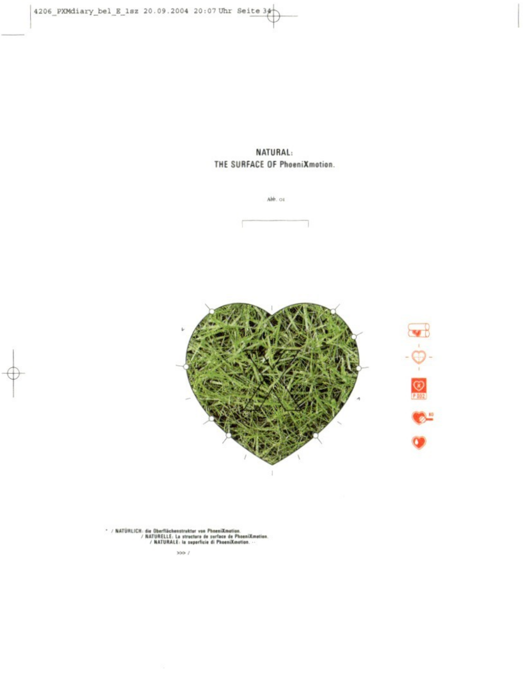

ABB. 03

° / NATÜRLICH: die Oberflächenstruktur von PhoeniXmotion.
/ NATURELLE: La structure de surface de PhoeniXmotion.
/ NATURALE: la superficie di PhoeniXmotion. °°
>>> /

BRILLIANT:
THE PRINT PERFORMANCE OF PhoeniXmotion.

ABB. 04

° / BRILLANT: die Druckeigenschaften von PhoeniXmotion.
/ REMARQUABLE: Les propriétés d'impression de PhoeniXmotion.
/ BRILLANTE: la performance di stampa di PhoeniXmotion. °°
>>> /

ASCENT

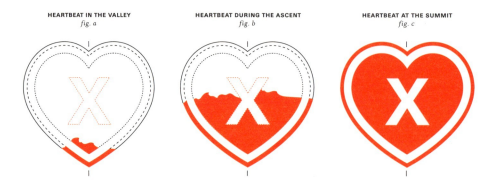

HEARTBEAT IN THE VALLEY
fig. a

HEARTBEAT DURING THE ASCENT
fig. b

HEARTBEAT AT THE SUMMIT
fig. c

PhoeniXmotion (2)

LOWER BLOOD PRESSURE, GREATER HEARTBEAT.

AUFSTIEG / ASCENSION / SALITA

WENIGER BLUTDRUCK, MEHR HEARTBEAT -- MOINS DE TENSION, PLUS DE BATTEMENT DE CŒUR -- PIÙ BASSA È LA PRESSIONE SANGUIGNA, PIÙ FORTE BATTE IL TUO CUORE --
>>> /

FIG A) heartbeat im Tal / battement de cœur dans la vallée / battito del cuore a valle
FIG B) heartbeat beim Aufstieg / battement de cœur lors de l'ascension / battito del cuore durante la scalata
FIG C) heartbeat an der Spitze / battement de cœur au sommet / battito del cuore sulla vetta

15.3 /

Diary
CLIENT _ SCHEUFELEN PAPERS

(2006)

BOOK OF
INDEPENDENCE

The fan base of the Heartbeat diaries had grown to a five-figure number, all of whom couldn't possibly be visited in the run-up to Christmas. So we came up with the *Book of Independence* – and as a radical consequence we became independent of time. The calendar consisted of empty pages and a sheet of stickers with days, weeks and months that could be stuck in according to personal whim. As such, it is just as conceivable for the diary to start on your own birthday as it is to have a complete year without appointments on a Friday. To further boost sales, the *Book of Independence* was also available from bookshops from the very start. The best Amazon review:
»*Brilliant book – a must-have. The only strange thing is that it keeps referring to a paper factory every now and then. Perhaps there is some form of surreptitious advertising going on here?*«.

Die Fangemeinde der Heartbeat Diaries war inzwischen auf eine fünfstellige Zahl gewachsen, die unmöglich alle kurz vor Weihnachten besucht werden konnten. Also erfanden wir das *Book Of Independence* – und machten uns in radikaler Konsequenz unabhängig von der Zeit. Das Kalendarium bestand aus leeren Seiten und einem Stapel Aufkleberbogen mit Tages, Wochen- und Monatsangaben, die man ganz nach Gusto selbst einkleben konnte: So ist der Beginn des Diary am eigenen Geburtstag genauso denkbar wie ein ganzes Jahr ohne Termine an einem Freitag. Eine weitere Hilfe für den Vertrieb: Das *Book Of Independence* gab es von Anfang an auch über den Buchhandel. Die schönste Amazon-Rezension:
»*Geiles Buch – unbedingt kaufen. Komisch nur, dass da hin und wieder von einer Papierfabrik die Rede ist. Vielleicht ist da Schleichwerbung im Spiel?*«.

FREE YOUR LIFE
JUST BE!

THE BOOK OF INDEPENDENCE

/ in four chapters:
BIRTH -- SCHOOL -- WORK -- ETERNITY

>>> /

-- *fig. 01* --

BIRTH

/ STEP ONE /

/ Mit dem ersten Atemzug erkennt der Mensch die eigene Unabhängigkeit:
Das Leben beginnt mit dem Schrei nach Freiheit.

// With the first breath, a human being recognises his or her independence: Life begins with a cry for freedom. //
Avec son premier souffle, l'être humain reconnaît sa propre indépendance :
la vie commence par le cri de la liberté. //...

{CHAPTER I}

X   -- *time is yours*

BE FREE! [|_|]

: This book is your own personal diary of independence.

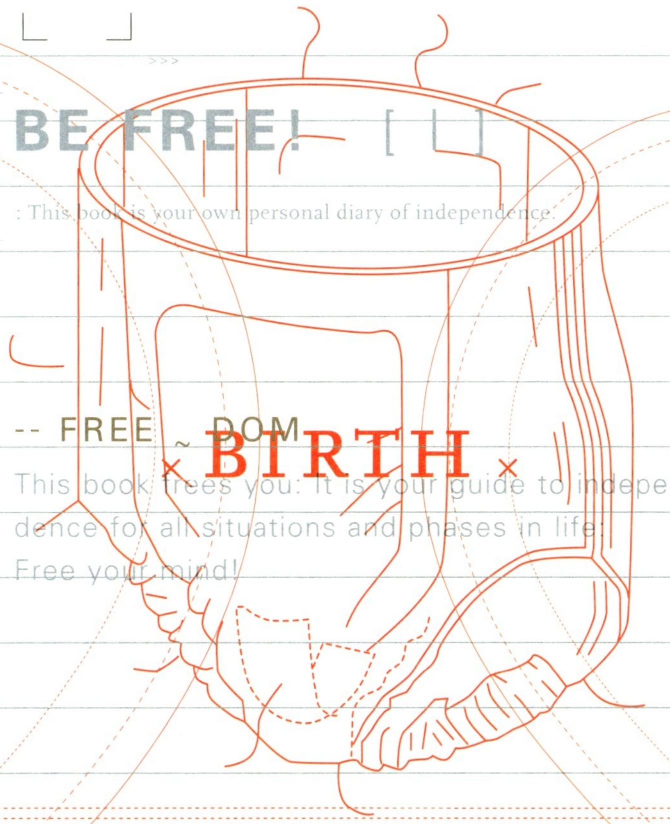

-- FREE ~ DOM BIRTH x

This book frees you: It is your guide to independence for all situations and phases in life.
Free your mind!

SCHEUFELEN PROUDLY PRESENTS:
THE BOOK OF INDEPENDENCE

-- FREE ~ PERSONAL SPACE

IN 1848, CARL SCHEUFELEN WAS DISMISSED FROM CIVIL SERVICE DUE TO ‚DEMOCRATIC
ACTIVITIES' – AND FOUNDED THE PAPIERFABRIK SCHEUFELEN. PAPER HAS ALWAYS BEEN THE
SPACE FOR AN UNOBSTRUCTED DEVELOPMENT OF INDEPENDENCE AND FREEDOM. TO THE PRESENT
DAY, THE PAPIERFABRIK SCHEUFELEN HAS REMAINED DIFFERENT: INDEPENDENT FOR 150 YEARS
NOW - WITH INNOVATION AS A TRADITION AND A GLOBAL PRESENCE WHEREVER EXTRAORDINARY
THOUGHTS REQUIRE AN EXTRAORDINARY BASE. THE PAPER FOR YOUR PERSONAL DECLARATION

>>> /

become independent: /step1   you are here
                                |
                                1 2 3 4

WORK

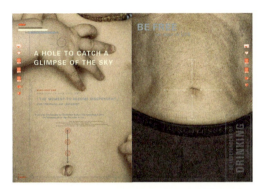 

16.0 /

GOOD DESIGN IS HUMAN.

.16

.16

The only measure of good design is the human being. We are both the originators and the audience. The formal principles of good design are those of the body, the functional ones those of the mind and the aesthetic ones those of the heart. Good design is profoundly human. Its most vital aspiration is sustainability; its most appealing effect is a smile. Bad design is the expression of poor self-awareness and a lack of respect.

Der einzige Maßstab für gutes Design ist der Mensch. Er ist stets Absender und Zielgruppe zugleich. Formale Gesetzmäßigkeiten guter Gestaltung sind die des Körpers, funktionale die des Geistes, ästhetische die des Herzens. Gutes Design ist zutiefst menschlich. Sein wichtigster Anspruch ist Nachhaltigkeit, seine schönste Wirkung ein Lächeln. Schlechtes Design ist Ausdruck mangelnder Selbsterkenntnis und fehlenden Respekts.

16.1 /

Annual Report
CLIENT _ METRO GROUP

(2010)

/ THE WORK OF _ STRICHPUNKT /

THE WORLD OF
PAOLO

Even for the activities of a large corporation there is a binding element between markets and brands: people. And of those, every single one is ultimately special. That is why we didn't talk about millions of anonymous customers in the METRO GROUP annual report, but just one: Paolo, the trattoria owner from Rome, and a typical day in his life. In similar fashion the following year we visited a sales assistant in Shanghai and listened to her whilst she sang karaoke.

Auch für die Aktivitäten eines Großkonzerns gibt es ein verbindendes Element zwischen Märkten und Marken: die Menschen. Und davon ist jeder letztlich ganz besonders. Weshalb wir im Report der METRO Group nicht über Millionen anonymer Kunden berichteten, sondern nur über einen einzigen: den Trattoria-Besitzer Paolo aus Rom und einen ganz normalen Tag in seinem Leben. Im Jahr darauf besuchten wir dann ebenso exemplarisch eine Verkäuferin in Shanghai und hörten ihr beim Karaoke-Singen zu.

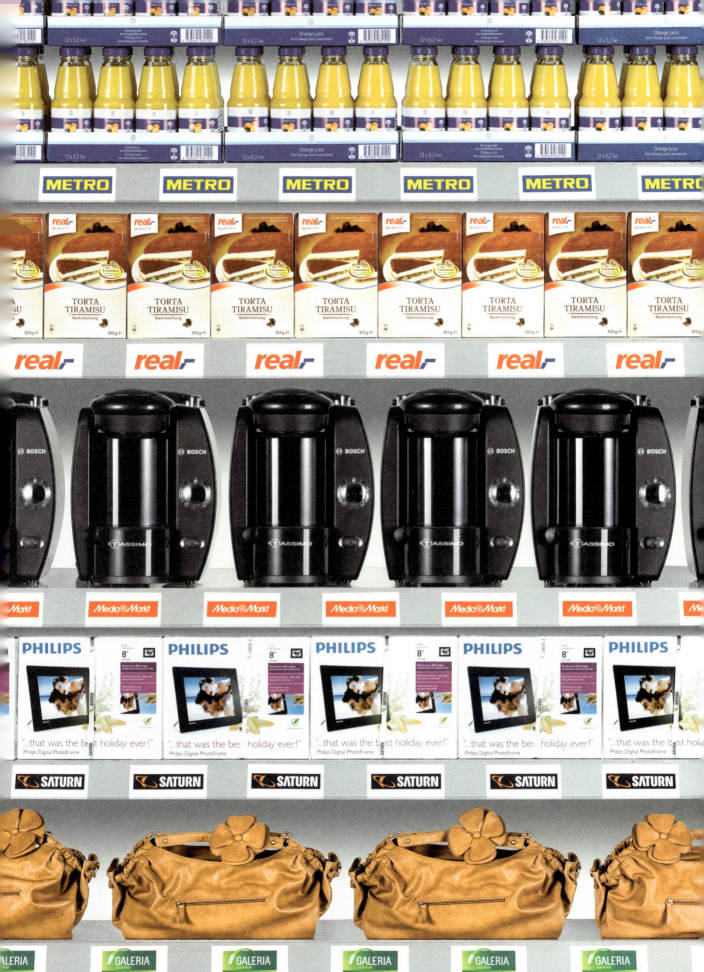

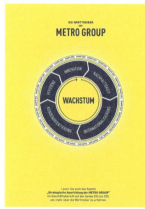
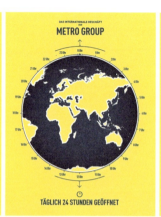
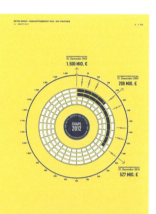

Alles für Paolo – 9 von 36.400 Produkten

Das Produktangebot der Metro Cash & Carry Großmärkte umfasst frisches Obst und Gemüse, regionale Spezialitäten sowie eine große Auswahl an Eigenmarken. Diese wurden 2009 vollständig neu ausgerichtet, um Profikunden noch besser in ihrem Tagesgeschäft zu unterstützen. So gibt es spezielle Eigenmarken für Hotellerie und Gastronomie ebenso wie preisgünstige Artikel und Premium-Produkte von Metro Cash & Carry. Für Paolo Allegrini bedeutet das: Er spart beim Einkauf Geld, ohne Abstriche bei der Qualität machen zu müssen.

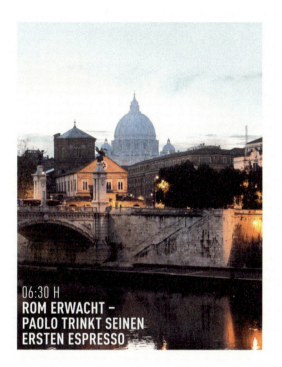

06:30 H
**ROM ERWACHT –
PAOLO TRINKT SEINEN
ERSTEN ESPRESSO**

07:15 H
**LUIGI BRINGT DIE FRISCHEN BLUMEN,
PAOLO IST LÄNGST AUF DEM WEG
ZU METRO CASH & CARRY**

09:15 H
**SCHNELL AUSGEPACKT,
DIE KÜCHENCREW
WARTET SCHON**

10:15 H
**DANIELA STEHT
AUF RÖMISCHE
KLASSIKER**

**GÜLAY LIEBT
PAOLO ALLEGRINIS
HÜFTGOLD**

14:45 H
**ANTONIO
– STEPPTÄNZER, SÄNGER UND SEIT
FAST 20 JAHREN STAMMGAST**

**GIANCARLO
IST DER
CHEF AM HERD**

**KLEINE PAUSE
KURZ VOR MITTERNACHT –
GIOVANNI DREHT AUF**

02:00 H
**KÜCHE GEPUTZT,
EIN LETZTER CAPPUCCINO
– FINITO!**

16.2 /

Packaging
CLIENT _ STRICHPUNKT

(2006)

SILENT NIGHT
HOLY NIGHT

When design ideas make people smile and think at the same time, then a great deal has already been achieved. For a Christmas fundraising campaign we put 300 Christmas records bought from a boot sale into transparent sleeves with the title *Silent Night – Holy Night* to bring to mind the hearing impaired people for whom Christmas really is a very, very silent occasion.

Wenn Designideen Menschen gleichzeitig zum Lächeln und zum Nachdenken bringen, ist schon viel erreicht. Für eine Weihnachts-Spendenaktion steckten wir 300 Weihnachts-Schallplatten vom Flohmarkt in eine transparente Hülle mit der Aufschrift *Silent Night – Holy Night* und erinnerten damit an die gehörlosen Menschen, für die Weihnachten tatsächlich ein sehr, sehr stilles Fest ist.

WORK

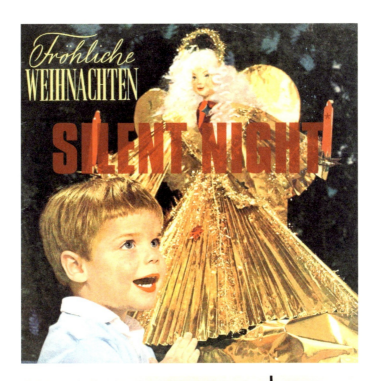

WORK

WORK

17.0 /

GOOD DESIGN IS EXCITING.

.17

The rest pulse is the designer's death. Only the tangible heartbeat of the creator is capable of inducing positive vibrations in the user: good design is stimulating and exciting. Relaxation only produces concepts that are destined for the drawer, tired, overworked standards and oversaturated trivia. There is nothing worse than a nice project. Every good piece of design harbours the desire for triumphant success or resounding failure. There is nothing in between.

Der Ruhepuls ist der Tod des Designers. Nur der spürbare Herzschlag des Gestalters erzeugt positive Schwingungen beim Nutzer: Gutes Design regt an und auf. Entspannt entstehen nur Schubladenkonzepte, müde Standards und saturierte Belanglosigkeiten.
Nichts ist schlimmer als ein nettes Projekt. In jedem guten Stück Design steckt der Wunsch nach absoluter Begeisterung oder grandiosem Scheitern. Dazwischen ist nichts.

17.1 /

Editorial Design
CLIENT _ ART DIRECTORS CLUB

(2005)

/ THE WORK OF _ STRICHPUNKT /

GO FOR
GOLD

Exciting design comes into being when you consistently pursue an idea. It doesn't get any easier when, of all things, the remit asks you to design a book with the 400 best ideas of the year. One insight did help us in this respect: every advertiser would climb over dead bodies to get their hands on a gold award from the ART DIRECTORS CLUB. Just like the days of yore in the Wild West. That is why the yearbook exudes gold rush fever, from the cover with the ADC sheriff's badge to the *Wanted* posters for the individual categories. When it came to the personal showdown at the presentation of the book, we had a little surprise up our sleeves for the jury: we presented the concept of our competitor Kurt Weidemann – and vice versa. The outcome: both concepts were triumphant and were used one after the other for two years.

Aufregendes Design entsteht, wenn man eine Idee konsequent verfolgt. Das wird nicht einfacher, wenn der Auftrag ausgerechnet lautet, ein Buch mit den 400 besten Ideen des Jahres zu gestalten. Eine Erkenntnis half uns dabei weiter: Für die Gold-Awards des Art Directors Club geht jeder Werber über Leichen. Ganz wie damals im Wilden Westen. Und deshalb atmet das Jahrbuch vom Einband mit ADC-Sheriffstern bis zu den Wanted-Plakaten für die einzelnen Kategorien Goldgräberstimmung. Um dem persönlichen Showdown bei der Präsentation des Buches zu umgehen, hatten wir eine kleine Überraschung für die Jury parat: Wir präsentierten das Konzept unseres Mitbewerbers Kurt Weidemann – und umgekehrt. Das Ergebnis: Beide Konzepte siegten und wurden in zwei Jahren nacheinander umgesetzt.

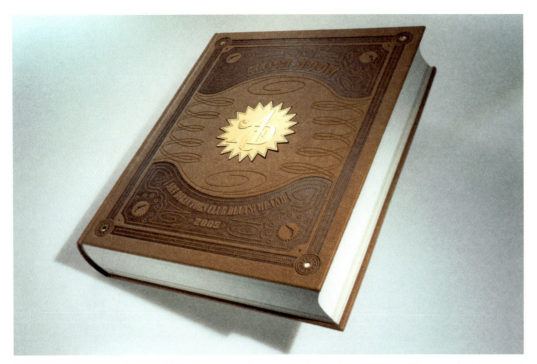

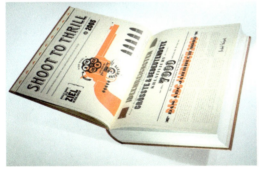

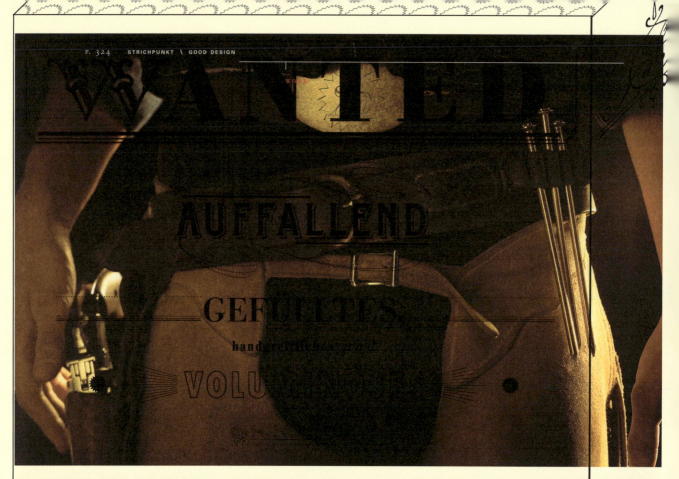

DER ADC *belohnt mit:*

einem bronzenen ADC Nagel

...und...

2 Auszeichnungen!

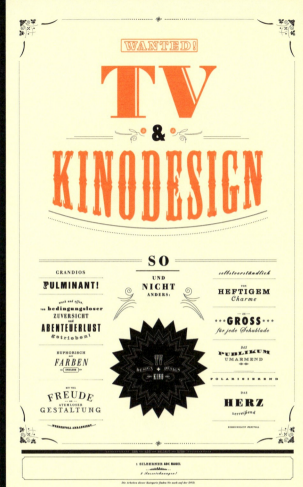

!!!WANTED!!!

DAS

COURAGIERTESTE,
artikulierteste,
PRÄGNANTESTE

CD

CORPORATE DESIGN

(Ganzheitliches Erscheinungsbild)

BELOHNUNG

2 SILBERNE + 1 BRONZENER ADC NAGEL + 5 Auszeichnungen!

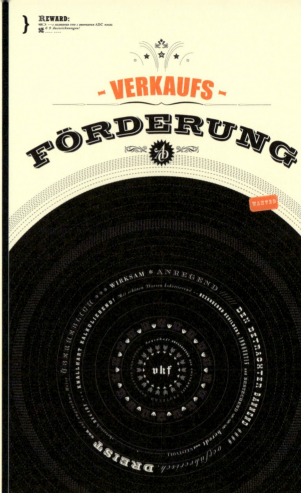

~ VERKAUFS ~
FÖRDERUNG

REWARD

DER ADC BRINGT SIE AUF STREIFE:
DEUTSCHLANDS VORZEIGBARSTE
PUBLIKUMS
ANZEIGEN

DIE ERGREIFUNG

·· REICHLICH ··

BELOHNT!

SILBERNE UND BRONZENE NÄGEL.
FÜR DEN EHRLICHEN FINDER:

FOCUS

WANTED!

Die
LEISESTEN & LAUTESTEN,
ungewöhnlichsten,
WIRKSAMSTEN,
ERGREIFENDSTEN
und
REVOLUTIONÄRSTEN

PLAKATE
~ UND POSTER ~

(INDOOR UND OUTDOOR)

!!!

BELOHNUNG:

HÄNGT SIE!

Es wir vergibt 6 Nägel:

WANTED

AUFFALLEND

GEFÜLLTES,
handgreifliches und
VOLUMINÖSES

PACKUNGS-
DESIGN

ERGREIFT DAS PACK!

WANTED

DER ADC MACHT SICH NICHT AUFT SONST:

DIE
VISIONÄRSTEN,
leckersten,
UNVORHERSEHBARSTEN,
UNSERE SINNE am süßesten
BETÖRENDEN,
SCHÖPFERISCHSTEN

TV *spots*

BELOHNUNG:
2 SILBERNE + 2 BRONZENE
NÄGEL

MOST WANTED

beschaulichsten, ABGEDREHTESTEN, befriedigendsten

— PASSIONIERTESTEN —

MUSIK VIDEOS

REWARD

WANTED!

UNBESTECHLICHSTEN, ANSEHNLICHSTEN, VIELVERSPRECHENDSTEN

Filme

VERKAUFSFÖRDERUNG & UNTERNEHMENSDARSTELLUNGEN

MOST WANTED!

LEBENDIGE, PASSIONIERTE, SCHWATZHAFTE und EXZENTRISCHE

FUNK SPOTS

Der ADC warnt vor: FUNKTIONIERENDEN EMPFÄNGERN!

MOST WANTED

DIGITALE MEDIEN

NORMEN DURCHBRECHEND

FREUDE VERHEISSEND

TAGES ZEITUNGS **ANZEIGEN**

AUFREGEND, AUFFALLEND ATTRAKTIV

GNADENLOS UNTERHALTSAM

WANTED

kommunikativste und erfreulichste *Reaktionen* HERVORRUFENDE

DIALOG MARKETING

MAILINGS und ANZEIGEN

WANTED!

DIALOGMARKETING KAMPAGNEN

sinnlich BERÜHREND, ÜBERZEUGEND, AUSDRUCKSSTARK

AUF DEN **PUNKT GEBRACHT**

WANTED!

Wohltönend harmonisch, *beseelt* ..GEHÖRIG TOSEND..

MUSIKKOMPOSITIONEN & SOUNDDESIGN

REWARD

WANTED

DIE ATEMBERAUBENDSTEN, STIMMUNGSVOLLSTEN und EINGÄNGIGSTEN

EVENTS

DER ADC FEIERT JEDE FESTSETZUNG!

MOST WANTED

A-Z

TEXT

TÄTERPROFIL:

!REWARD!

MOST WANTED!

schräge Typen

MIT ... ONE DURCHSCHUSS:

TYPO-GRAFIE

FEST-SETZEN WIRD BELOHNT:

Der ADC warnt:

SCHRIFT STICHT ins AUGE!

PUBLIKUMS ANZEIGEN

LAUFENDER KAMPAGNEN

Ausdauer, *KAMPFESLUST,* AUSDRUCKSSTÄRKE, WITZ Geist.

Wanted!

18.0 /

GOOD DESIGN HURTS.

.18

.18

Visual intelligence is a mighty sword in the struggle against convention.
Good design is a quick, direct incision in the open heart of the beholder.
Creating something new means ignoring the familiar, breaking rules, offending visual sensibilities.
New ideas need birthing pains, the sharp rejection and mass ignorance.

Visuelle Intelligenz ist ein scharfes Schwert im Kampf gegen Konventionen.
Gutes Design ist der schnelle, direkte Schnitt ins offene Herz des Betrachters.
Neues gestalten heißt Gewohntes ignorieren, Regeln brechen, Sehgewohnheiten verletzen.
Das Neue braucht den Schmerz der Geburt, die Schärfe der Ablehnung,
die Ignoranz der Masse.

18.1 /

Event Design

CLIENT _ ART DIRECTORS CLUB GERMANY

(2008)

/ THE WORK OF _ STRICHPUNKT /

CREATIVE
SUMMIT

To give the newly created SUMMIT OF CREATIVITY congress format a strong image, we converted the points on the venerable ADC star into a summit ridge, combining visual codes from the world of mountains and thus perfectly emphasising the leading status of the ADC – well, we thought so anyway. For some upright advocates of a purer form of corporate design, however, treating the visual identity of the legendary club in such bold fashion was the pinnacle of insolence.

Um dem neu geschaffenen Kongressformat *Gipfel der Kreativität* einen starken Auftritt zu verschaffen, verwandelten wir die Zacken des altehrwürdigen ADC-Sterns in einen Gipfelgrat. Dazu geselle sich visuelle Chiffren aus der Bergwelt und machten so den Führungsanspruch des ADC auf zünftige Art und Weise deutlich – fanden wir zumindest. Für manche wackere Vertreter der reinen Lehre im Corporate Design war der freche Umgang mit dem Erscheinungsbild des legendären Clubs dennoch der Gipfel.

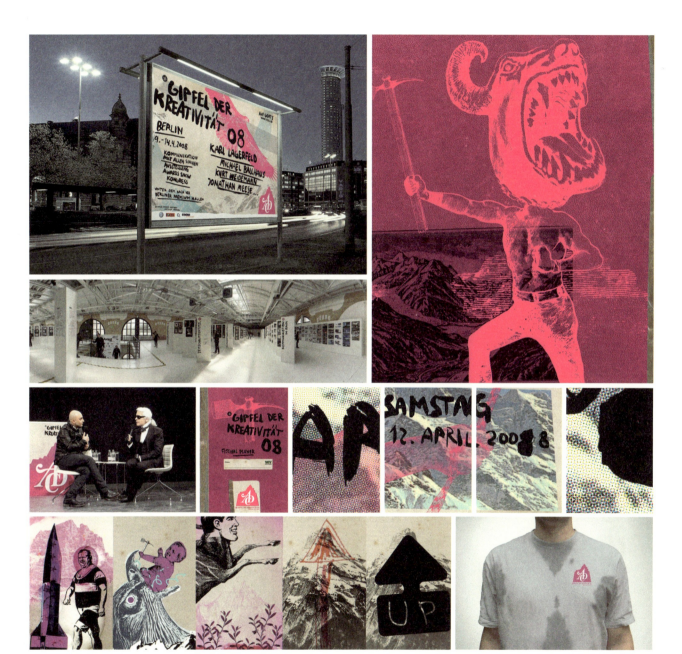

RSTAG
RIL 2008

18.2 /

Corporate Design
CLIENT _ ART DIRECTORS CLUB

(2009)

ADC _
NAIL THEM

Advertisers often have a low opinion of corporate design – because it limits their artistic freedom. This is taken to the extreme when it comes to the corporate design of a creative association. If you really want to make enemies for life, come up with a CD for 600 CDs. You can be sure that nobody will like it, anyone could have done it better, and everybody will do everything they can to shoot it down in flames. We wanted to make it as hard as possible for our clients to do that, so we took the ADC Nail – the trophy of the most important creative competition in Germany – and painted it bronze, silver, gold and the club's colours, black and magenta, thus boarding up every opportunity for other creative professionals to deface or disfigure it with their own ideas and tastes, us included *(see 18.1).*

Werber halten oft wenig von Corporate Design – weil es sie in ihrer gestalterischen Freiheit einschränkt. Auf die Spitze getrieben wird das, wenn es um das Corporate Design eines Kreativverbandes geht. Wenn du dir wirklich Feinde fürs Leben machen willst, gestalte ein CD für 600 CDs. Du kannst sicher sein: Keiner mag es, alle hätten es besser gekonnt, und jeder wird alles dafür tun, es zu torpedieren. Das wollten wir unseren Auftraggebern möglichst schwer machen und haben deshalb den ADC-Nagel – die Trophäe des größten deutschen Kreativwettbewerbs – in Bronze, Silber, Gold und den Hausfarben Schwarz und Magenta eingefärbt und alles damit zugebrettert, was andere Kreative mit Einzelideen je nach Geschmack ge- oder verunstalten könnten, uns selbst eingeschlossen *(siehe 18.1).*

**To ensure that the half-life of the corporate design is as long as possible,
we have packaged the basic elements into a daunting formula that nobody but us can actually understand.**
Um eine möglichst lange Halbwertszeit des Corporate Designs zu gewährleisten, haben wir die Grundzutaten in einer
einschüchternden Formel verpackt, die außer uns eigentlich niemand verstehen kann.

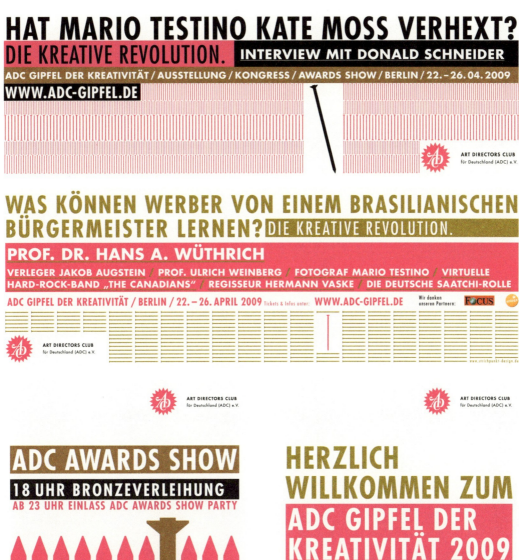

19.0 /

GOOD DESIGN IS NOTHING WITHOUT A GOOD IDEA.

.19

Content needs structure in order to be discernible for other people. Good design is more than just a vehicle: it is the formal expression of a creative idea that fuses harmoniously with the content. It is only in this way that you can appeal to a person's brain and heart. Without content, design is nothing more than an exercise in cavity sealing: without the creative idea, it remains ineffective.

Inhalt braucht Form, um für andere Menschen erfassbar zu werden. Gutes Design ist dabei mehr als Transportweg: Es ist formaler Ausdruck einer kreativen Idee, die sich mit dem Inhalt harmonisch verbindet. Nur so erreichst du neben dem Hirn auch den Bauch. Ohne Inhalt ist Design nur Hohlraumversiegelung, ohne gestalterische Idee bleibt es wirkungslos.

19.1 /

Annual Report
CLIENT _ 4MBO INTERNATIONAL ELECTRONIC AG

(2003)

/ THE WORK OF _ STRICHPUNKT /

MESSAGE IN A
BAG

4MBO markets high-tech products at low-cost prices via supermarkets *(see also chapter 4.2)*. We showcased the most important clients of 4MBO by using the classic means of portraying their image and products: the plastic bag. To the names of the clients we added terms from the business world and consequently outlined the business year (CapitAL DIvidend, PLUS point, NORMAlity, etc.). By punching a hole through the body of the book we also gave the entire annual report a carrying handle – and put it in a plastic bag.

4MBO vermarktet Hightechprodukte zu Billigpreisen über Supermärkte *(siehe auch Kap. 4.2)*. Wir zeigten die wichtigsten Kunden von 4MBO anhand ihres klassischen Image- und Produktträgers: der Plastiktüte. Die Namen der Kunden ergänzten wir zu Begriffen aus dem Wirtschaftsleben und erläuterten damit das Geschäftsjahr (KapitALDIenst, PLUSpunkt, NORMAlität etc.). Den gesamten Geschäftsbericht versahen wir per Stanzung durch den Buchblock ebenfalls mit einem Tragegriff – und steckten ihn in eine Plastiktüte.

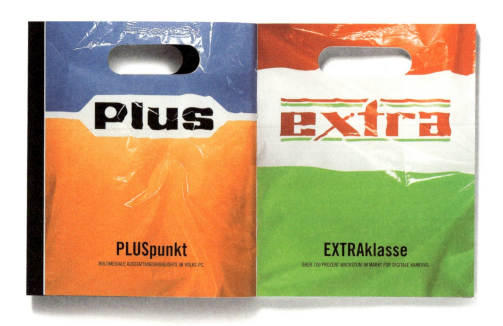

19.2 /

Branding
CLIENT _ SOLARWORLD

(2008 - 2011)

HERE COMES THE
SUN

For SOLARWORLD we came up with the slogan *sun at work*. Because wherever the sun shines, it is doing a successful job for Solarworld – and making Solarworld successful. We put people in the picture with images from around the world – from Mali to Times Square and even on the roof of the Audience Hall in the Vatican, where the solar installation ensures that the energy for the eternal light comes directly from the boss.

Für Solarworld erfanden wir den Claim *Sun At Work*. Denn überall, wo die Sonne scheint, macht sie erfolgreiche Arbeit für Solarworld – und Solarworld erfolgreich. Das haben wir weltweit ins Bild gesetzt – in Mali genauso wie am Times Square und auf dem Dach der Audienzhalle des Vatikans. Denn dort sorgt eine Solaranlage dafür, dass im Vatikan die Energie für das ewige Licht direkt vom Chef kommt.

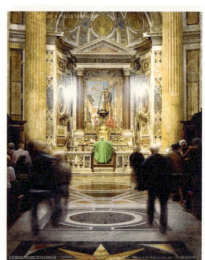

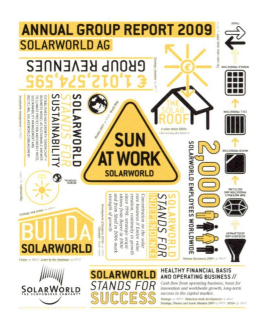

19.3 /

Corporate Design

CLIENT _ VERLAG HERMANN SCHMIDT MAINZ

(2002)

REPORT OF
ANNUAL REPORTS

Strichpunkt not only designs brands, but also lots of annual reports. If it isn't a report for Mercedes, Metro or Merck (they also come from us), it can be pretty exhausting trying to explain at length what the company actually does produce – and the reason why our report is so well suited to it. So we came up with the idea of designing annual reports for names that everybody knows. As a result, 24 reports were produced for Adam and Eve and Buffalo Bill, Casanova and Donald Duck, the Mafia and Karl Marx, Count Dracula and Father Christmas. From that came an exhibition, from the exhibition came our first book, and the book provided the basis for some genuine companies to charge us with the task of producing their annual report.

Strichpunkt gestaltet nicht nur Marken, sondern auch eine Menge Geschäftsberichte. Wenn es nicht gerade Reports für Mercedes, Metro oder Merck sind (die kommen auch von uns), ist es mitunter ganz schön anstrengend, langatmig zu erklären, was die Firma eigentlich herstellt – und warum deshalb unser Report so gut dazu passt. Also kamen wir auf die Idee, Geschäftsberichte für Unternehmen zu gestalten, die jeder kennt. So entstanden 24 Reports für Adam und Eva und Buffalo Bill, Casanova und Donald Duck, die Mafia und Karl Marx, Graf Dracula und den Nikolaus. Daraus wurde eine Ausstellung, aus der Ausstellung unser erstes Buch und das Buch der Grund für manches echte Unternehmen, uns mit seinem Bericht zu beauftragen.

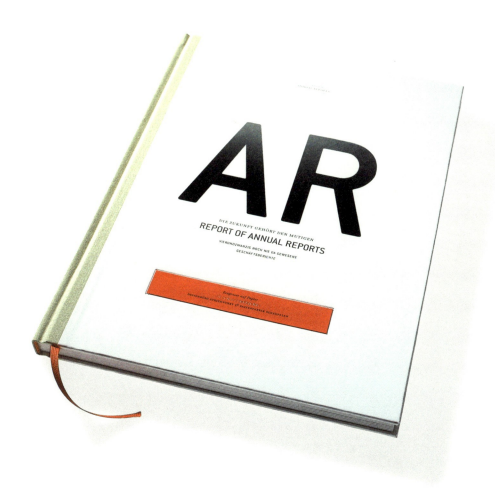

Annual reports for Martin Luther / Protestantism plc (a startup from 1514); Bayern Munich,
Louis Braille, the inventor of Braille embossed printing; Buffalo Bill and the mafia.
Geschäftsberichte für Martin Luthers Protestantismus AG (ein Start-up von 1514), Bayern München, Louis Braille,
den Erfinder der Blindenschrift, für Buffalo Bill und die Mafia.

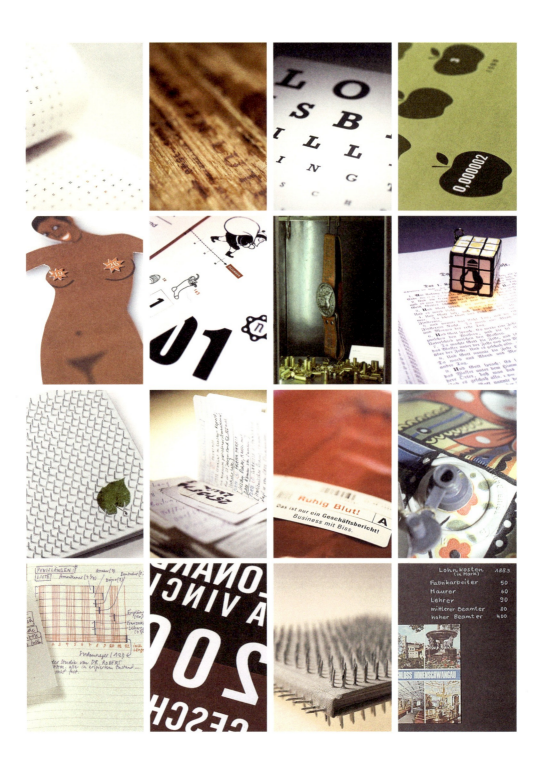

20.0 /

GOOD DESIGN IS OVER-RATED.

.20

Good design is indispensable. Good design creates beauty, riches and fame. Good design is inspiring, personal fulfilment and a way of making the world a better place. In your role as a good designer, you invest all your thoughts, feelings and actions in creating something good. But remember to remain a human among humans, to laugh, to love, to live and to experience. If you are a good designer, good design is important to you – but many other things are far more important.

Gutes Design ist unverzichtbar. Gutes Design macht schön, reich und berühmt. Gutes Design inspiriert, ist persönliche Erfüllung und ein Weg, die Welt zu verbessern. Als guter Designer legst du dein ganzes Denken, Fühlen und Handeln kompromisslos in gute Gestaltung. Aber vergiss nie, darüber hinaus Mensch unter Menschen zu bleiben, zu lachen, zu lieben, zu leben, zu erleben. Wenn du ein guter Designer bist, ist dir gute Gestaltung wichtig – und dennoch vieles andere viel wichtiger.

Jochen Rädeker / Kirsten Dietz

KIRSTEN DIETZ > studied visual communication at the Stuttgart State Academy of Art and Design. Besides her work for Strichpunkt she has been a juror at the Cannes Lions, ADC Europe, New York Festivals, Hong Kong Design Biennale, ADC Deutschland, red dot Award and many more. Kirsten brings her dog to the office and likes to be anywhere but Stuttgart.

KIRSTEN DIETZ > hat visuelle Kommunikation an der Kunstakademie Stuttgart studiert. Neben der Arbeit bei Strichpunkt war sie Jurorin bei den Cannes Lions, ADC Europe, New York Festivals, Hong Kong Design Biennale, ADC Deutschland, red dot Award u.v.a. Kirsten bringt ihren Hund mit ins Büro und ist gerne überall, nur nicht in Stuttgart.

JOCHEN RÄDEKER > also studied visual communication at the Stuttgart State Academy of Art and Design. Besides his work for Strichpunkt, since 2009 he has been spokesman of the board for the Art Directors Club Germany, giving talks, holding lectures and sitting on juries. At work he likes listening to AC/DC, Tenacious D and John Watts.

JOCHEN RÄDEKER > hat ebenfalls visuelle Kommunikation an der Kunstakademie Stuttgart studiert. Neben der Arbeit bei Strichpunkt ist er seit 2009 Vorstandssprecher des Art Directors Club für Deutschland, hält Vorträge, lehrt und juriert. Bei der Arbeit hört er gerne AC/DC, Tenacious D und John Watts.

The minutes of our first strategy meeting consisted of one small note. Written on it was our name: Strichpunkt. And two sentences.
The first: 'Within three years we want to be one of the ten best design agencies in Germany.' The second: 'The future belongs to the brave.'
The first was achieved quicker than we imagined, and the aspiration soon changed to that of becoming one of the world's leading designers.
The second can be found on our business cards to this day – because we still believe in it, with every new project.

What became of the idea of Kirsten Dietz and Jochen Rädeker wanting to stand in for each other whilst one of them was on holiday?
An agency was born that is now among the largest design studios in Germany.
What became of the goal of winning just one TDC award in our lifetime? We have now won so many that we have stopped counting.
What became of the aspiration of realising projects with which we were completely happy and satisfied?
Nothing. There is always something that we feel we perhaps could have done better or differently.
That is why we are delighted with every new customer we get. That is why we still get fired up for every new project.
That is why there is nothing we like better than working through the night with fantastic colleagues and making the pizza delivery
service rich. That is why we are still as enthusiastic about designing as we were 15 years ago.
That is why this book is not a retrospective, but a standpoint.

Das Protokoll unseres ersten Strategiemeetings bestand aus einem kleinen Zettel.
Auf dem stand unser Name: Strichpunkt.
Und zwei Sätze.
Der erste: »Wir wollen innerhalb von drei Jahren zu den zehn besten Designagenturen Deutschlands gehören«.
Der zweite: »Die Zukunft gehört den Mutigen«.
Das Erste hat schneller geklappt, als wir dachten, und wurde schnell zum Anspruch, weltweit zu den führenden Gestaltern zu gehören.
Das Zweite steht bis heute auf unseren Visitenkarten – denn daran glauben wir immer noch, bei jedem neuen Projekt.

Aus der Idee, dass Kirsten Dietz und Jochen Rädeker sich gegenseitig im Urlaub vertreten wollten, ist eine Agentur geworden,
die zu den größten deutschen Designbüros zählt. Aus dem Ziel, einmal im Leben mit einem TDC-Award ausgezeichnet zu werden,
sind so viele Auszeichnungen geworden, dass wir aufgehört haben, sie zu zählen.
Aus dem Anspruch, Projekte zu realisieren, mit denen wir rundum glücklich und zufrieden sind, ist nichts geworden:
Es gibt immer noch etwas, was man anders und vielleicht besser hätte machen können.
Deshalb freuen wir uns auf jeden neuen Kunden. Deshalb brennen wir für jedes neue Projekt.
Deshalb gibt es nichts Spannenderes, als mit tollen Kollegen die Nacht zum Tag und den Pizzaservice reich zu machen.
Deshalb sind wir heute noch so begeisterte Gestalter wie vor 15 Jahren.
Deshalb ist dieses Buch keine Retrospektive, sondern ein Standpunkt.

THE WORLD OF STRICHPUNKT DESIGN

staff developement /

0.1 /

1996 --
02

2003 --
16

2011 --
40

THE WORLD OF STRICHPUNKT DESIGN

working process /

0.2 /

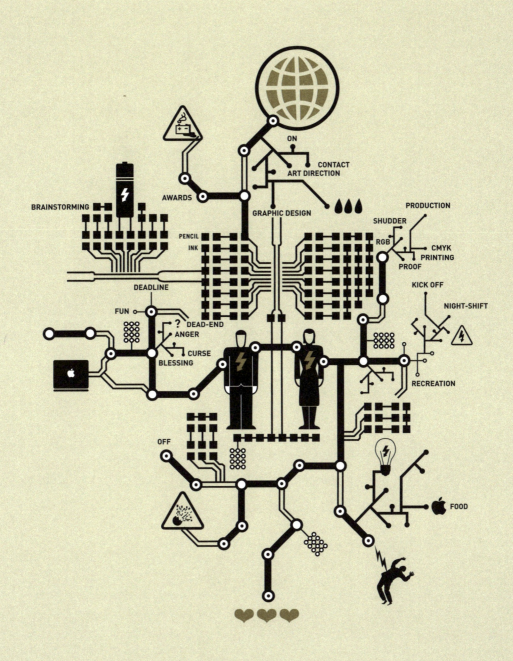

THE WORLD OF STRICHPUNKT DESIGN

how to keep in touch /

0.3 /

STRICHPUNKT-DESIGN.COM

BLOG.STRICHPUNKT-DESIGN.DE

TWITTER.COM/STRICHPUNKT

FACEBOOK.COM/STRICHPUNKTDESIGN

STRICHPUNKT-DESIGN.DE

YOUTUBE.COM/USER/STRICHPUNKTDESIGN

THE WORLD OF STRICHPUNKT DESIGN
awards /

0.4 /

CREATIVITY AWARDS
IN MAJOR INTERNATIONAL CONTESTS

2001 - 2011

*

AMONG THEM:
> 30 AWARDS FROM THE TYPE DIRECTORS CLUB OF NEW YORK
RED DOT AGENCY OF THE YEAR
ADC DESIGN AGENCY OF THE YEAR
MULTIPLE ADC GOLDS, RED DOT GRANDS PRIX,
NY FESTIVAL GRANDS PRIX, HOW DESIGN BEST OF SHOW
AND MANY MORE.

THE WORLD OF STRICHPUNKT DESIGN

working storage /

0.5 /

some stuff to store

DATA STORAGE EQUIPMENT USED BY STRICHPUNKT

(in gigabytes)

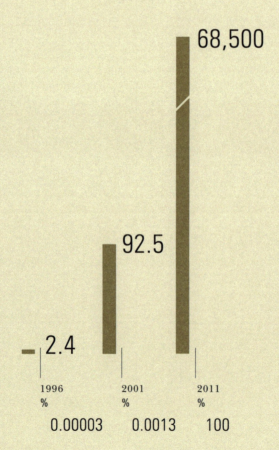

68,500

92.5

2.4

1996 %	2001 %	2011 %
0.00003	0.0013	100

THE WORLD OF STRICHPUNKT DESIGN

projects _ gender /

0.6 /

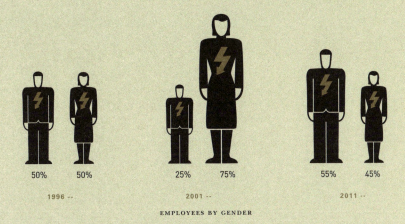

| 50% | 50% | | 25% | 75% | | 55% | 45% |

1996 --   2001 --   2011 --

EMPLOYEES BY GENDER

1996 --   2000 --   2011 --
32   **90**   **480**

SINGLE PROJECTS PER YEAR (ACCORDING TO JOB NUMBERS)

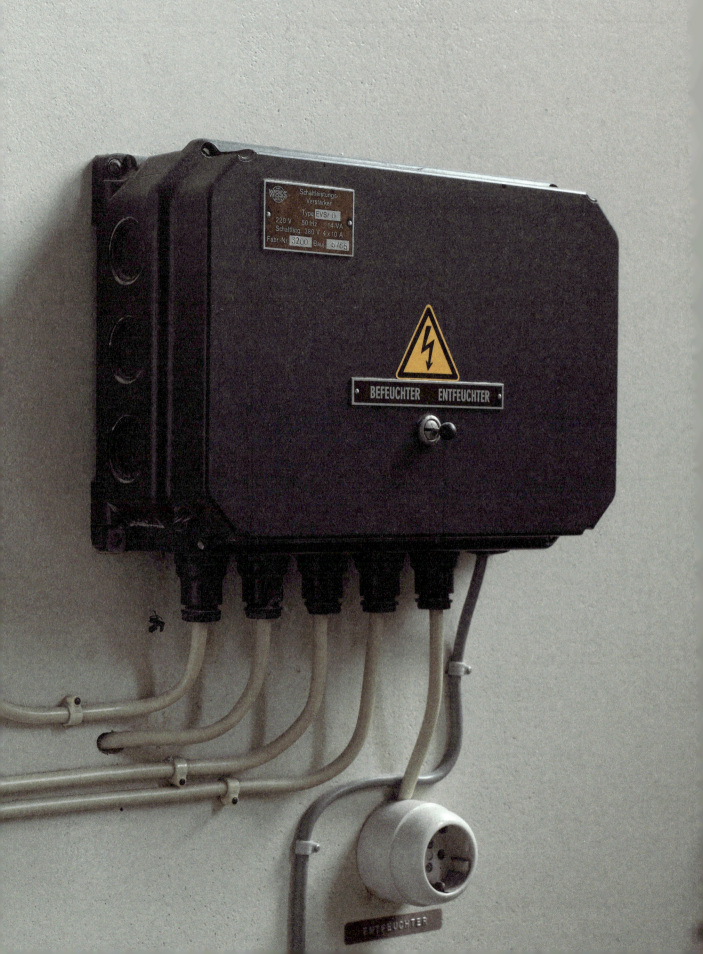

HAUPTSCHALTER

**Vorsicht !
Lebensgefahr !**
Trennschalter nur
bei ausgeschaltetem
Leistungsschalter betätigen !

**Hochspannung
Vorsicht !
Lebensgefahr**

IDEAS

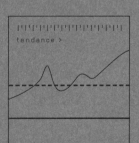

tendance >

IMPACT   **SYMPATHY**   **SURPRISE**

ON / OFF

IDEA LISM

 ## 0...12 V

**Those who only have
a job to do
-- /
just stay away**

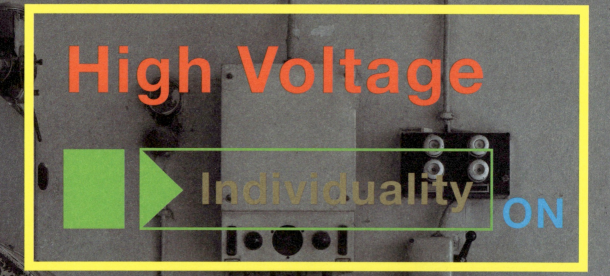

High Voltage

▶ Individuality ON

Low Voltage

▶ Standard off

Think   or   deliver.   ------
Create   or   copy   and   paste.   --------
Be innovative, be yourself and be proud of it, or do what
anybody does. -----------------------------------

---------------------------   ▶ **DECIDE**

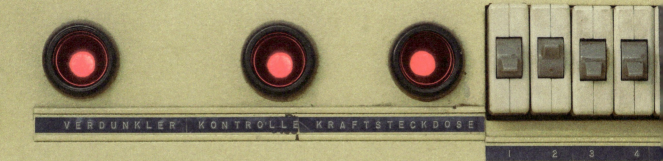

VERDUNKLER | KONTROLLE KRAFTSTECKDOSE

1 2 3 4

HELLER   HALT   DUNKLER

```
SICHERUNGEN -- TOMATEN
VER.DUNKLER          NR.1
SPEISERAUM           NR.2
OBERGESCHOSS         NR.3
STECK.LINKS.HW.NR.4
       CLUBRAUM      NR.5 -   28
BAR                  NR.6 -   23
       HALLE         NR.7
LÜSTER-RECHTS  NR.8    -19-30
   LÜSTER-MITTE NR.9   -20-31
   LÜSTER-LINKS  NR.10 -21-32
WANDLAM.-SAAL  NR.11 U.NR.22
ANRICHTE             NR.12
    RESERVE          NR.13-   -16
    RESERVE          NR.24-27-29
STECKRECHTS.H  NR.14
KASSENSTECKDO..NR.15
STECKD.SA.LI.        NR.17
MASCHINENRAUM        NR.18
WANDLA.SAAL.LI.NR.22
SPEISERAUM           NR.25  -  26
STECKDO. SA.RE.NR.33
NR.34    AUFZUG
NR.35    VERDUNKLER
NR.36    GR.KAFFEEMASCHINE
NR.37    KRAFTSTECKDOSE
```

HAUPTSCHALTER

CONTROL MONITOR ▶ CLOSE ▶ PRINT

High Voltage

 ▶ Locate **ON**

Project Management

 RUN OK
 NO INJECT

Strategy

 ▶ Locate **01**

Super Access

Visible Values   YES

Men at Work   Normal

Design

▶ Locate **02**

Idea Alarm

 ▶ Control **03**

Technical

▶ Control

Branding
Reporting
Image Building

▶ ▶ ▶ **SUBMIT**

Progress

DANGER

⚡ 380 V

Never stop thinking – never stop moving!

IDEA

60005981 000

Entriegelung
Lüftung

H 2

S

H 3

T

B O I

Friedens + Schutzfall

Wartur
Turnus:
13 w
Anlagenn
VC
geprüft
Datum

A I A

Hauptschalter
nur bei Gefahr
ausschalten

Those who only believe in market research have
no room for vision. People with a high regard for
standards have no room for individual solutions.
Those who do everything exactly the way everyone
considers to be correct have no room for
innovations.

Phase L1

Kältemaschine 3

Wartung
Kältemaschine 3

Erdschlußüberwachung 24 V	220 V	Steuerspannung fehlt	Si.-Automat ausgelöst	Kreislauf 1	Kreislauf 2	Kaltwasser Temp.	Kurbelwannen- heizung

Kompressor									Maschinenleistung	
1	2	3	4	5	6	7	8	75 %	87,5 %	100 %

Grundfreigabe 3	Start-Freigabe Maschine 3	Betriebsbereit	Spannungsversorg. Schrank-Kälte	Sonderbetrieb	Kältemaschine in Automatik

Kältemaschine 3

It's more about
HEAVY THINKING
than pretty pictures.

THE STRICHPUNKT TEAM 1996 – 2011

you'll never walk alone /

0.7 /

Design is teamwork. Good design is good teamwork.
The quality of the projects featured in this book would not have been nearly half as good without the many superb minds who contributed
their thoughts, designs and hard work, and helped to present, produce and critique. This book is your book:

Design ist Teamwork. Gutes Design ist gutes Teamwork.
Keines der in diesem Buch abgebildeten Projekte wäre auch nur annähernd in dieser Qualität entstanden, wenn nicht viele großartige Köpfe mitgedacht,
mitgestaltet, mitgearbeitet, mitpräsentiert, mitproduziert, mitkritisiert, mitkorrigiert und mitgefiebert hätten. Dieses Buch ist Euer Buch:

Anders Bergesen	Sabrina Grimm	Denise Kaufmann	**Sabine Müller**	Marc Schergel	Tina Werner
Elke Bertsch	Selina Gruler	Sandra Kimmel	Ulli Neutzling	Carolin Schilling	**Nicola Wetzel**
Katja Betzler	Stefanie Hartmann	**Monika Kobylecka**	**Tobias Nusser**	**Sibylle Schupp**	Felix Widmaier
Christopher Biel	**Jan Hartwig**	**Jeannette Kohnle**	**Julia Ochsenhirt**	Andrea Seebauer	Thomas Wieland
Salome Birkhofer	**Karin Häußermann**	Ulrike Krebs	Michaela Ortlieb	Volker Stegmaier	**Andrea Witke**
Reinhard Blessing	Niels Heinemann	Jürgen Kreitmeier	Sarah Owens	**Fred Stern**	Agnetha Wohlert
Daniel Bretzmann	**Francis Hippel**	**Silke Krieg**	Patricia Peckels	Tanja Stetter	**Christine Wolf**
Philipp Brune	Steffen Hoenicke	**Thomas Langanki**	Uta Pressler	**Alexandra Storr**	**Tatjana Wolfram**
David Claaßen	**Peter Hoppe**	Teresa Lindenmayer	Andreas Pfetzing	Philipp Strayle	Julia Worbs
Katja Deml	**Susanne Hörner**	Jan Maier	**Nicole Pfletschinger**	**Melanie Stuwe**	**Nico Wüst**
Marcus Dünkel	Tina Hornung	Anika Marquardsen	Michael Reinhardt	**Jochen Theurer**	**Barbara Zecha**
Günter Eizenhöfer	**Annabel Huml**	Niko Mayer	Uli Sackmann	Jeannine Urban	**Stephanie Zehender**
Beate Flamm	Heike Jassmann	Petra Michel	Christine Schaal	Rene Vogt	**Sinco Zheng**
Caroline Fritz	Holger Jungkunz	**Anja Mittelstädt**	Melanie Schäfer	Gernot Walter	Oliver Zügel
Ludwika Galczynska	Christoph Kalscheuer	Michael Moser	Stephan Schenk	Markus Weissenhorn	

bold type > actual staff

IMPRINT

CONCEPT, TEXT AND DESIGN // Kirsten Dietz & Jochen Rädeker
The copyright for the projects depicted in this book is held by
Strichpunkt Design and the respective clients.
The copyright for the images featured in the
projects is held by the photographers concerned.

HIGH VOLTAGE PHOTOS // Niels Schubert
PROJECT PHOTOS // Nicola Lazi and Strichpunkt Design
PORTRAIT OF DIETZ/RÄDEKER // Tom Ziora
REPRODUCTION, IMAGE PROCESSING AND TYPESETTING //
Strichpunkt Design
FONTS // Century Schoolbook and Univers.
PAPER // Munken Polar 105 g/qm, FSC
PRINTER // Appl, Wemding
BOOKBINDER // Schaumann, Darmstadt
COVER // Leissing, Landau

STRICHPUNKT DESIGN
// Stuttgart office:
Krefelder Straße 32 _ 70376 Stuttgart
// Berlin office:
Die Hackeschen Höfe
Sophienstraße 6 _ 10178 Berlin

phone +49 (0)711 620 3270
info@strichpunkt-design.de
www.strichpunkt-design.de
facebook: strichpunktdesign
twitter: strichpunkt
youtube: strichpunktdesign
vimeo: highvoltage

VERLAG HERMANN SCHMIDT MAINZ
Robert-Koch-Straße 8 _ 55129 Mainz
phone +49 (0)6131 506 030 _ fax +49 (0)6131 506 080
info@typografie.de
www.typografie.de
facebook: Hermann Schmidt Verlag
twitter: VerlagHSchmidt

ISBN 978-3-87439-827-5
Printed in Germany.